50 Vegetarian Desserts Recipes for Home

By: Kelly Johnson

Table of Contents

- Chocolate Avocado Mousse
- Berry Parfait
- Lemon Bars
- Apple Crisp
- Mango Sorbet
- Pumpkin Pie
- Coconut Macaroons
- Banana Bread
- Carrot Cake
- Almond Butter Cups
- Raspberry Cheesecake
- Blueberry Cobbler
- Key Lime Pie
- Fig Newtons
- Peanut Butter Cookies
- Watermelon Granita
- Orange Chocolate Truffles
- Pineapple Upside-Down Cake
- Cinnamon Rolls
- Chia Seed Pudding
- Pistachio Ice Cream
- Cranberry Orange Scones
- Strawberry Shortcake
- Date Balls
- Blackberry Crumble
- Pecan Pie Bars
- Oatmeal Raisin Cookies
- Maple Walnut Fudge
- Cherry Almond Tart
- Lemon Poppy Seed Cake
- Coconut Rice Pudding
- Espresso Brownies
- Salted Caramel Pretzel Bark
- Apple Turnovers
- Gingerbread Cookies

- Apricot Bars
- Tiramisu
- Mint Chocolate Chip Ice Cream
- Nutella Crepes
- Chocolate Covered Strawberries
- Kiwi Lime Pie
- Pomegranate Panna Cotta
- Mocha Cheesecake Bars
- Banana Cream Pie
- Raspberry Chocolate Tart
- Lemon Thyme Shortbread
- Pineapple Coconut Cupcakes
- Pistachio Baklava
- Mango Sticky Rice
- S'mores Dip

Chocolate Avocado Mousse

Ingredients:

- 2 ripe avocados
- 1/2 cup cocoa powder (unsweetened)
- 1/2 cup maple syrup or agave syrup (adjust to taste)
- 1 teaspoon vanilla extract
- Pinch of salt
- Optional toppings: fresh berries, shaved chocolate, or chopped nuts

Instructions:

1. **Prepare the Avocados:**
   - Cut the avocados in half, remove the pits, and scoop the flesh into a food processor or blender.
2. **Blend the Ingredients:**
   - Add cocoa powder, maple syrup or agave syrup, vanilla extract, and a pinch of salt to the avocados.
3. **Blend Until Smooth:**
   - Blend all ingredients together until smooth and creamy. Scrape down the sides of the blender or food processor as needed to ensure everything is well combined.
4. **Chill (Optional):**
   - For a firmer texture, transfer the mousse to a bowl or individual serving dishes and chill in the refrigerator for at least 30 minutes before serving.
5. **Serve:**
   - Spoon the chocolate avocado mousse into serving bowls or glasses. Garnish with fresh berries, shaved chocolate, or chopped nuts if desired.
6. **Enjoy:**
   - Serve and enjoy this decadent and healthier chocolate dessert!

Tips:

- Adjust the sweetness to your preference by adding more or less maple syrup or agave syrup.
- For extra smoothness, you can use a high-powered blender or food processor.
- This mousse can be stored in the refrigerator for up to 2-3 days. Cover tightly with plastic wrap or transfer to an airtight container.

This Chocolate Avocado Mousse is not only delicious but also packed with healthy fats from the avocado and antioxidants from the cocoa powder, making it a guilt-free treat for any occasion!

Berry Parfait

Ingredients:

- 1 cup Greek yogurt or dairy-free yogurt alternative
- 1 cup mixed berries (such as strawberries, blueberries, raspberries)
- 1/2 cup granola (homemade or store-bought)
- 1 tablespoon honey or maple syrup (optional)
- Fresh mint leaves, for garnish (optional)

Instructions:

1. **Prepare the Berries:**
    - Wash the berries thoroughly and pat them dry. If using strawberries, hull and slice them into smaller pieces.
2. **Assemble the Parfait:**
    - In serving glasses or bowls, start by layering a spoonful of Greek yogurt (or dairy-free alternative) at the bottom.
3. **Add Berries:**
    - Next, add a layer of mixed berries on top of the yogurt.
4. **Sprinkle Granola:**
    - Sprinkle a layer of granola over the berries.
5. **Repeat Layers:**
    - Repeat the layers of yogurt, berries, and granola until the glasses are filled or until you've used up all the ingredients.
6. **Drizzle with Honey or Maple Syrup (Optional):**
    - If desired, drizzle a little honey or maple syrup over the top of the parfait for added sweetness.
7. **Garnish:**
    - Garnish with fresh mint leaves for a pop of color and extra freshness.
8. **Serve:**
    - Serve immediately and enjoy this delicious and nutritious Berry Parfait!

Tips:

- You can customize your parfait by adding different fruits, nuts, or seeds between the layers.
- For a vegan version, use dairy-free yogurt and skip honey or use a plant-based sweetener.
- Prepare the parfait ahead of time and refrigerate until ready to serve.

This Berry Parfait is not only visually appealing but also a wonderful way to enjoy the natural sweetness and nutritional benefits of fresh berries and yogurt!

Lemon Bars

Ingredients:

For the Crust:

- 1 cup all-purpose flour
- 1/4 cup granulated sugar
- 1/2 cup unsalted butter, softened

For the Lemon Filling:

- 1 cup granulated sugar
- 2 large eggs
- 1/4 cup all-purpose flour
- 1/2 teaspoon baking powder
- 1/4 cup fresh lemon juice (about 2 lemons)
- 1 tablespoon lemon zest (optional)

For Dusting:

- Powdered sugar (optional)

Instructions:

1. **Preheat the Oven:**
   - Preheat your oven to 350°F (175°C). Grease an 8x8 inch baking pan or line it with parchment paper.
2. **Prepare the Crust:**
   - In a medium bowl, mix together the flour and granulated sugar. Cut in the softened butter until the mixture is crumbly. Press the mixture evenly into the bottom of the prepared baking pan.
3. **Bake the Crust:**
   - Bake the crust in the preheated oven for about 15-20 minutes, or until lightly golden. Remove from the oven and set aside.
4. **Prepare the Lemon Filling:**
   - In another medium bowl, whisk together the granulated sugar and eggs until smooth. Add the flour and baking powder, and whisk until well combined. Stir in the fresh lemon juice and lemon zest (if using).
5. **Pour the Filling:**
   - Pour the lemon filling over the pre-baked crust, spreading it out evenly.

6. **Bake the Lemon Bars:**
   - Return the pan to the oven and bake for an additional 20-25 minutes, or until the filling is set and slightly golden around the edges. The center should not jiggle when the pan is gently shaken.
7. **Cool and Dust with Powdered Sugar:**
   - Allow the lemon bars to cool completely in the pan. Once cooled, dust with powdered sugar if desired.
8. **Cut and Serve:**
   - Cut into squares or bars and serve. Store any leftovers in an airtight container in the refrigerator.

Tips:

- For a stronger lemon flavor, increase the amount of lemon zest used in the filling.
- For a gluten-free version, substitute the all-purpose flour with a gluten-free flour blend.
- Ensure the lemon bars are fully cooled before cutting to get clean edges.

Enjoy these tangy and sweet Lemon Bars as a refreshing dessert that's perfect for any occasion!

Apple Crisp

Ingredients:

For the Filling:

- 6 cups apples, peeled, cored, and sliced (about 6 medium apples)
- 1 tablespoon lemon juice
- 1/2 cup granulated sugar
- 1/2 teaspoon ground cinnamon
- 1/4 teaspoon ground nutmeg (optional)
- 1 tablespoon all-purpose flour

For the Topping:

- 1 cup old-fashioned rolled oats
- 1/2 cup all-purpose flour
- 1/2 cup packed brown sugar
- 1/2 teaspoon ground cinnamon
- 1/4 teaspoon salt
- 1/2 cup unsalted butter, melted

Instructions:

1. **Preheat the Oven:**
   - Preheat your oven to 350°F (175°C). Grease a 9x13 inch baking dish or a similarly sized dish.
2. **Prepare the Filling:**
   - In a large bowl, toss the sliced apples with the lemon juice. Add the granulated sugar, ground cinnamon, ground nutmeg (if using), and all-purpose flour. Mix well to coat the apples evenly. Pour the apple mixture into the prepared baking dish and spread it out evenly.
3. **Prepare the Topping:**
   - In a separate bowl, combine the rolled oats, all-purpose flour, packed brown sugar, ground cinnamon, and salt. Add the melted butter and stir until the mixture is well combined and crumbly.
4. **Assemble the Apple Crisp:**
   - Sprinkle the oat mixture evenly over the apples in the baking dish.
5. **Bake the Apple Crisp:**
   - Bake in the preheated oven for 40-45 minutes, or until the topping is golden brown and the apples are tender and bubbly.

6. **Cool and Serve:**
    - Allow the apple crisp to cool slightly before serving. Serve warm, optionally with a scoop of vanilla ice cream or a dollop of whipped cream.

Tips:

- For a gluten-free version, substitute the all-purpose flour with a gluten-free flour blend.
- You can mix different types of apples for a more complex flavor, such as using a combination of tart Granny Smith and sweet Honeycrisp apples.
- Add a handful of chopped nuts, such as pecans or walnuts, to the topping mixture for extra crunch.

Enjoy this delicious and comforting Apple Crisp as a delightful dessert that brings the flavors of autumn to your table!

Mango Sorbet

Ingredients:

- 4 ripe mangoes, peeled and pitted
- 1/2 cup sugar (adjust to taste)
- 1/2 cup water
- 2 tablespoons lime juice
- 1 teaspoon lime zest (optional)
- Pinch of salt

Instructions:

1. **Prepare the Simple Syrup:**
    - In a small saucepan, combine the sugar and water. Heat over medium heat, stirring until the sugar is completely dissolved. Remove from heat and let the simple syrup cool to room temperature.
2. **Prepare the Mangoes:**
    - Cut the mangoes into chunks and place them in a blender or food processor.
3. **Blend the Ingredients:**
    - Add the cooled simple syrup, lime juice, lime zest (if using), and a pinch of salt to the blender with the mango chunks. Blend until the mixture is smooth and well combined.
4. **Chill the Mixture:**
    - Pour the mango mixture into a large bowl or container, cover, and refrigerate for at least 2-3 hours or until thoroughly chilled.
5. **Churn the Sorbet:**
    - Once the mixture is chilled, pour it into an ice cream maker and churn according to the manufacturer's instructions. This usually takes about 20-25 minutes, depending on your machine.
6. **Freeze the Sorbet:**
    - Transfer the churned sorbet to an airtight container and freeze for at least 2-3 hours or until firm.
7. **Serve:**
    - Scoop the mango sorbet into bowls or cones and serve immediately. Garnish with fresh mint leaves or lime slices if desired.

Tips:

- If you don't have an ice cream maker, you can pour the mango mixture into a shallow dish and freeze it. Every 30 minutes, stir the mixture with a fork to break up ice crystals until it reaches a smooth, sorbet-like consistency (this process takes about 3-4 hours).
- Adjust the amount of sugar based on the sweetness of your mangoes and your personal preference.
- For a tropical twist, you can add a splash of coconut milk to the mixture before blending.

Enjoy this Mango Sorbet as a cool and refreshing treat, perfect for hot summer days or any time you crave a taste of the tropics!

Pumpkin Pie

Ingredients:

For the Crust:

- 1 1/4 cups all-purpose flour
- 1/2 teaspoon salt
- 1/2 cup unsalted butter, chilled and cut into small pieces
- 3-4 tablespoons ice water

For the Filling:

- 1 (15-ounce) can pumpkin puree
- 3/4 cup granulated sugar
- 1 teaspoon ground cinnamon
- 1/2 teaspoon ground ginger
- 1/4 teaspoon ground cloves
- 1/4 teaspoon ground nutmeg
- 1/2 teaspoon salt
- 2 large eggs
- 1 (12-ounce) can evaporated milk

Instructions:

1. **Prepare the Crust:**
    - In a medium bowl, combine the flour and salt. Cut in the chilled butter using a pastry blender or your fingers until the mixture resembles coarse crumbs.
    - Gradually add the ice water, one tablespoon at a time, mixing until the dough comes together. Form the dough into a disk, wrap it in plastic wrap, and refrigerate for at least 30 minutes.
2. **Roll Out the Crust:**
    - On a lightly floured surface, roll out the chilled dough to fit a 9-inch pie dish. Transfer the dough to the pie dish, trim any excess, and crimp the edges. Place the crust in the refrigerator while you prepare the filling.
3. **Preheat the Oven:**
    - Preheat your oven to 425°F (220°C).
4. **Prepare the Filling:**
    - In a large bowl, mix the pumpkin puree, granulated sugar, cinnamon, ginger, cloves, nutmeg, and salt until well combined.

        - Beat in the eggs. Gradually stir in the evaporated milk until the filling is smooth.
5. **Assemble the Pie:**
        - Pour the pumpkin filling into the prepared pie crust.
6. **Bake the Pie:**
        - Bake in the preheated oven for 15 minutes. Reduce the oven temperature to 350°F (175°C) and continue baking for an additional 40-50 minutes, or until a knife inserted near the center comes out clean.
        - If the crust starts to brown too quickly, cover the edges with aluminum foil to prevent burning.
7. **Cool and Serve:**
        - Allow the pie to cool on a wire rack for at least 2 hours. Serve chilled or at room temperature, topped with whipped cream if desired.

Tips:

- You can use store-bought pie crust for convenience.
- For a deeper flavor, consider using a mix of brown sugar and granulated sugar in the filling.
- Make sure to use pure pumpkin puree, not pumpkin pie filling, for this recipe.

Enjoy this classic Pumpkin Pie as a delightful and comforting dessert, perfect for holiday gatherings or any special occasion!

Coconut Macaroons

Ingredients:

- 4 cups sweetened shredded coconut
- 1 (14-ounce) can sweetened condensed milk
- 1 teaspoon vanilla extract
- 1/4 teaspoon salt
- 2 large egg whites
- 1/2 cup semi-sweet chocolate chips (optional, for drizzling or dipping)

Instructions:

1. **Preheat the Oven:**
    - Preheat your oven to 325°F (165°C). Line a baking sheet with parchment paper or a silicone baking mat.
2. **Mix the Ingredients:**
    - In a large mixing bowl, combine the shredded coconut, sweetened condensed milk, vanilla extract, and salt. Mix until all the ingredients are well incorporated.
3. **Whip the Egg Whites:**
    - In a separate bowl, beat the egg whites with an electric mixer on high speed until stiff peaks form.
4. **Fold in the Egg Whites:**
    - Gently fold the beaten egg whites into the coconut mixture until fully combined. Be careful not to deflate the egg whites too much.
5. **Scoop the Macaroons:**
    - Using a small cookie scoop or a tablespoon, scoop out portions of the mixture and place them onto the prepared baking sheet, spacing them about 1 inch apart.
6. **Bake the Macaroons:**
    - Bake in the preheated oven for 20-25 minutes, or until the macaroons are golden brown around the edges and set in the middle.
7. **Cool the Macaroons:**
    - Allow the macaroons to cool on the baking sheet for a few minutes before transferring them to a wire rack to cool completely.
8. **Optional Chocolate Drizzle or Dip:**
    - If desired, melt the chocolate chips in a microwave-safe bowl in 30-second intervals, stirring after each interval until smooth. Drizzle the melted

chocolate over the cooled macaroons or dip the bottoms of the macaroons into the chocolate. Place them on parchment paper to set.
9. **Serve:**
    - Serve the coconut macaroons once the chocolate has set (if using). Store any leftovers in an airtight container at room temperature for up to a week.

Tips:

- Make sure to use sweetened shredded coconut for the best texture and sweetness.
- For added flavor, you can also mix in 1/2 teaspoon of almond extract with the vanilla extract.
- If you prefer a chewier texture, slightly underbake the macaroons, but ensure they are set enough to hold their shape.

Enjoy these delightful Coconut Macaroons, a perfect treat for any coconut lover and an easy addition to your dessert repertoire!

Banana Bread

Ingredients:

- 1 cup granulated sugar
- 1/2 cup unsalted butter, softened
- 2 large eggs
- 1 teaspoon vanilla extract
- 1 1/2 cups all-purpose flour
- 1 teaspoon baking soda
- 1/2 teaspoon salt
- 1/2 cup sour cream
- 1 cup mashed ripe bananas (about 2-3 bananas)
- 1/2 cup chopped nuts (optional)
- 1/2 cup chocolate chips (optional)

Instructions:

1. **Preheat the Oven:**
   - Preheat your oven to 350°F (175°C). Grease a 9x5-inch loaf pan or line it with parchment paper.
2. **Cream the Butter and Sugar:**
   - In a large mixing bowl, cream the softened butter and granulated sugar together until light and fluffy.
3. **Add the Eggs and Vanilla:**
   - Beat in the eggs one at a time, making sure each is fully incorporated before adding the next. Stir in the vanilla extract.
4. **Mix the Dry Ingredients:**
   - In a separate bowl, whisk together the all-purpose flour, baking soda, and salt.
5. **Combine Wet and Dry Ingredients:**
   - Gradually add the dry ingredients to the butter mixture, mixing until just combined.
6. **Add Sour Cream and Bananas:**
   - Fold in the sour cream and mashed bananas until the batter is smooth. If using, gently fold in the chopped nuts and/or chocolate chips.
7. **Pour the Batter:**
   - Pour the batter into the prepared loaf pan and spread it evenly.
8. **Bake the Banana Bread:**

- Bake in the preheated oven for 60-70 minutes, or until a toothpick inserted into the center comes out clean. If the top starts to brown too quickly, cover it loosely with aluminum foil.
9. **Cool the Bread:**
    - Allow the banana bread to cool in the pan for about 10 minutes, then transfer it to a wire rack to cool completely.
10. **Serve:**
    - Slice and serve the banana bread warm or at room temperature. Enjoy it plain or with a spread of butter.

Tips:

- Overripe bananas with brown spots are best for banana bread as they are sweeter and more flavorful.
- For added texture and flavor, consider adding a teaspoon of cinnamon or a pinch of nutmeg to the dry ingredients.
- Banana bread can be stored in an airtight container at room temperature for up to 3 days or refrigerated for up to a week. It also freezes well for up to 3 months.

Enjoy this classic Banana Bread recipe, a comforting and delightful treat that's perfect for breakfast, a snack, or dessert!

Carrot Cake

Ingredients:

For the Cake:

- 2 cups all-purpose flour
- 2 teaspoons baking powder
- 1 1/2 teaspoons baking soda
- 1 teaspoon salt
- 2 teaspoons ground cinnamon
- 1/2 teaspoon ground nutmeg
- 1/2 teaspoon ground ginger
- 1 1/2 cups granulated sugar
- 1/2 cup brown sugar, packed
- 1 cup vegetable oil
- 4 large eggs
- 2 teaspoons vanilla extract
- 3 cups grated carrots (about 4-5 medium carrots)
- 1 cup chopped walnuts or pecans (optional)
- 1/2 cup raisins (optional)

For the Cream Cheese Frosting:

- 8 ounces cream cheese, softened
- 1/2 cup unsalted butter, softened
- 4 cups powdered sugar
- 1 teaspoon vanilla extract
- 1-2 tablespoons milk (optional, for consistency)

Instructions:

1. **Preheat the Oven:**
    - Preheat your oven to 350°F (175°C). Grease and flour two 9-inch round cake pans or line them with parchment paper.
2. **Prepare the Dry Ingredients:**
    - In a medium bowl, whisk together the flour, baking powder, baking soda, salt, cinnamon, nutmeg, and ginger. Set aside.
3. **Mix the Wet Ingredients:**

- In a large mixing bowl, combine the granulated sugar, brown sugar, and vegetable oil. Beat in the eggs, one at a time, until well incorporated. Stir in the vanilla extract.
4. **Combine Wet and Dry Ingredients:**
   - Gradually add the dry ingredients to the wet mixture, mixing until just combined.
5. **Fold in Carrots and Add-ins:**
   - Fold in the grated carrots, chopped nuts, and raisins (if using) until evenly distributed.
6. **Bake the Cake:**
   - Divide the batter evenly between the prepared cake pans. Bake in the preheated oven for 25-30 minutes, or until a toothpick inserted into the center comes out clean.
   - Allow the cakes to cool in the pans for about 10 minutes, then transfer them to a wire rack to cool completely.
7. **Prepare the Cream Cheese Frosting:**
   - In a large mixing bowl, beat the softened cream cheese and butter together until smooth and creamy. Gradually add the powdered sugar, one cup at a time, mixing until smooth. Stir in the vanilla extract.
   - If the frosting is too thick, add milk one tablespoon at a time until the desired consistency is reached.
8. **Frost the Cake:**
   - Place one cake layer on a serving plate and spread a layer of frosting on top. Place the second cake layer on top and frost the top and sides of the cake with the remaining frosting.
9. **Decorate (Optional):**
   - Decorate the cake with additional chopped nuts, shredded coconut, or carrot decorations if desired.
10. **Serve:**
    - Slice and serve the carrot cake. Store any leftovers in an airtight container in the refrigerator for up to a week.

Tips:

- For extra moisture, you can add 1/2 cup crushed pineapple (drained) to the batter.
- Make sure the cream cheese and butter are fully softened to avoid lumps in the frosting.

- Carrot cake can be made in advance and tastes even better the next day as the flavors meld.

Enjoy this delicious Carrot Cake, a perfect blend of warm spices, sweet carrots, and creamy frosting!

Almond Butter Cups

Ingredients:

For the Chocolate Layer:

- 1 1/2 cups semi-sweet chocolate chips or dark chocolate chips
- 1 tablespoon coconut oil

For the Almond Butter Filling:

- 1/2 cup almond butter
- 2 tablespoons coconut oil, melted
- 2 tablespoons maple syrup or honey
- 1/2 teaspoon vanilla extract
- Pinch of salt

Instructions:

1. **Prepare the Muffin Tin:**
   - Line a mini muffin tin with 12 paper liners. You can also use a regular muffin tin if you prefer larger almond butter cups.
2. **Make the Chocolate Layer:**
   - In a microwave-safe bowl, combine the chocolate chips and coconut oil. Microwave in 30-second intervals, stirring after each interval, until the chocolate is completely melted and smooth. Alternatively, you can melt the chocolate and coconut oil in a double boiler on the stove.
3. **Fill the Muffin Tin with Chocolate:**
   - Spoon a small amount of the melted chocolate into the bottom of each paper liner, just enough to cover the bottom. Place the muffin tin in the freezer for about 10 minutes to set the chocolate.
4. **Prepare the Almond Butter Filling:**
   - In a medium bowl, mix together the almond butter, melted coconut oil, maple syrup or honey, vanilla extract, and salt until smooth and well combined.
5. **Add the Almond Butter Filling:**
   - Remove the muffin tin from the freezer. Spoon a small amount of the almond butter mixture on top of the set chocolate layer in each paper liner, spreading it out slightly. Leave a little space at the top for the final chocolate layer.
6. **Top with Chocolate:**

- Spoon the remaining melted chocolate over the almond butter layer in each paper liner, covering the almond butter completely. Gently tap the muffin tin on the counter to smooth out the chocolate and remove any air bubbles.
7. **Set the Almond Butter Cups:**
    - Place the muffin tin back in the freezer for about 20-30 minutes, or until the almond butter cups are fully set.
8. **Serve:**
    - Once set, remove the almond butter cups from the muffin tin and peel off the paper liners. Store them in an airtight container in the refrigerator or freezer.

Tips:

- For a variation, you can use peanut butter, cashew butter, or sunflower seed butter in place of almond butter.
- To make the almond butter cups extra special, sprinkle a bit of sea salt on top of the chocolate layer before it sets.
- These almond butter cups can be stored in the refrigerator for up to 2 weeks or in the freezer for up to 3 months.

Enjoy these homemade Almond Butter Cups, a perfect combination of rich chocolate and creamy almond butter!

Raspberry Cheesecake

Ingredients:

For the Crust:

- 1 1/2 cups graham cracker crumbs
- 1/4 cup granulated sugar
- 1/2 cup unsalted butter, melted

For the Raspberry Sauce:

- 2 cups fresh or frozen raspberries
- 1/4 cup granulated sugar
- 1 tablespoon cornstarch
- 2 tablespoons water

For the Cheesecake Filling:

- 4 (8-ounce) packages cream cheese, softened
- 1 1/4 cups granulated sugar
- 1 teaspoon vanilla extract
- 4 large eggs
- 1/2 cup sour cream
- 1/2 cup heavy cream

Instructions:

1. **Preheat the Oven:**
    - Preheat your oven to 325°F (160°C). Grease a 9-inch springform pan or line the bottom with parchment paper.
2. **Make the Crust:**
    - In a medium bowl, combine the graham cracker crumbs, granulated sugar, and melted butter. Mix until the crumbs are evenly moistened.
    - Press the mixture firmly into the bottom of the prepared springform pan. Bake the crust for 10 minutes, then remove from the oven and let it cool while you prepare the filling.
3. **Prepare the Raspberry Sauce:**
    - In a small saucepan, combine the raspberries, granulated sugar, cornstarch, and water. Cook over medium heat, stirring frequently, until the mixture thickens and the raspberries break down, about 5-7 minutes.

- Strain the sauce through a fine-mesh sieve to remove the seeds. Set aside to cool.
4. **Make the Cheesecake Filling:**
   - In a large mixing bowl, beat the softened cream cheese and granulated sugar together until smooth and creamy.
   - Add the vanilla extract and mix until combined.
   - Add the eggs one at a time, beating well after each addition.
   - Mix in the sour cream and heavy cream until the batter is smooth and well combined.
5. **Assemble the Cheesecake:**
   - Pour half of the cheesecake filling over the cooled crust in the springform pan.
   - Spoon half of the raspberry sauce over the filling and swirl it gently with a knife or skewer.
   - Pour the remaining cheesecake filling over the raspberry layer.
   - Spoon the remaining raspberry sauce over the top and swirl it gently.
6. **Bake the Cheesecake:**
   - Place the springform pan in a large roasting pan. Pour hot water into the roasting pan to come about halfway up the sides of the springform pan (this is a water bath and helps prevent cracking).
   - Bake in the preheated oven for 55-65 minutes, or until the center is set but still slightly jiggly.
7. **Cool the Cheesecake:**
   - Turn off the oven and crack the door open. Let the cheesecake cool in the oven for 1 hour.
   - Remove the cheesecake from the water bath and let it cool completely at room temperature.
   - Refrigerate the cheesecake for at least 4 hours or overnight before serving.
8. **Serve:**
   - Remove the sides of the springform pan. Slice and serve the cheesecake chilled, garnished with fresh raspberries if desired.

Tips:

- Make sure all the ingredients are at room temperature for a smooth and creamy filling.
- Avoid overmixing the batter to prevent incorporating too much air, which can cause cracks.

- If you don't have a roasting pan, you can bake the cheesecake without the water bath, but be aware it may crack more easily.

Enjoy this decadent Raspberry Cheesecake, perfect for special occasions or whenever you're craving a rich and fruity dessert!

Blueberry Cobbler

Ingredients:

For the Blueberry Filling:

- 6 cups fresh or frozen blueberries
- 1 cup granulated sugar
- 1 tablespoon lemon juice
- 1/4 cup all-purpose flour
- 1 teaspoon vanilla extract
- 1/2 teaspoon ground cinnamon (optional)

For the Cobbler Topping:

- 1 cup all-purpose flour
- 1 cup granulated sugar
- 1 teaspoon baking powder
- 1/2 teaspoon salt
- 1/2 cup unsalted butter, melted
- 1 teaspoon vanilla extract
- 1/2 cup milk

Instructions:

1. **Preheat the Oven:**
   - Preheat your oven to 375°F (190°C). Grease a 9x13-inch baking dish or a deep-dish pie pan.
2. **Prepare the Blueberry Filling:**
   - In a large bowl, combine the blueberries, granulated sugar, lemon juice, flour, vanilla extract, and cinnamon (if using). Gently mix until the blueberries are evenly coated with the sugar and flour mixture.
3. **Pour the Filling into the Baking Dish:**
   - Transfer the blueberry mixture to the prepared baking dish, spreading it out evenly.
4. **Make the Cobbler Topping:**
   - In a medium bowl, whisk together the flour, sugar, baking powder, and salt.
   - Add the melted butter, vanilla extract, and milk. Stir until the batter is smooth and well combined.
5. **Assemble the Cobbler:**

- Spoon the cobbler batter over the blueberry filling, spreading it out as evenly as possible. The batter will spread as it bakes, so it doesn't need to completely cover the blueberries.
6. **Bake the Cobbler:**
    - Bake in the preheated oven for 40-45 minutes, or until the topping is golden brown and a toothpick inserted into the topping comes out clean.
7. **Cool the Cobbler:**
    - Allow the blueberry cobbler to cool for about 15 minutes before serving. This will help the filling set slightly.
8. **Serve:**
    - Serve the cobbler warm, with a scoop of vanilla ice cream or a dollop of whipped cream if desired.

Tips:

- If using frozen blueberries, there's no need to thaw them; just add a few extra minutes to the baking time.
- For an extra crunch, sprinkle some coarse sugar on top of the cobbler batter before baking.
- Feel free to mix in other berries like raspberries or blackberries for a mixed berry cobbler.

Enjoy this delicious Blueberry Cobbler, a comforting and sweet dessert that's perfect for any occasion!

Key Lime Pie

Ingredients:

For the Graham Cracker Crust:

- 1 1/2 cups graham cracker crumbs (about 10-12 whole graham crackers)
- 1/3 cup granulated sugar
- 1/2 cup unsalted butter, melted

For the Key Lime Pie Filling:

- 4 large egg yolks
- 1 can (14 ounces) sweetened condensed milk
- 1/2 cup freshly squeezed key lime juice (about 20-25 key limes)
- 1 tablespoon grated lime zest (optional)

For the Whipped Cream Topping:

- 1 cup heavy whipping cream
- 2 tablespoons powdered sugar
- 1/2 teaspoon vanilla extract

Instructions:

1. **Preheat the Oven:**
   - Preheat your oven to 350°F (175°C).
2. **Make the Graham Cracker Crust:**
   - In a medium bowl, combine the graham cracker crumbs, granulated sugar, and melted butter. Mix until the crumbs are evenly moistened.
   - Press the mixture firmly into the bottom and up the sides of a 9-inch pie dish.
   - Bake the crust in the preheated oven for 10 minutes. Remove from the oven and let it cool while you prepare the filling.
3. **Prepare the Key Lime Pie Filling:**
   - In a large mixing bowl, whisk the egg yolks until they are pale and fluffy.
   - Gradually add the sweetened condensed milk, whisking continuously until well combined.
   - Slowly add the key lime juice and lime zest (if using), whisking until smooth and creamy.
4. **Bake the Pie:**

- Pour the filling into the cooled graham cracker crust.
- Bake the pie in the preheated oven for 15-20 minutes, or until the filling is set but still slightly jiggly in the center.
- Remove the pie from the oven and let it cool to room temperature. Then refrigerate for at least 2 hours, or until fully chilled and set.

5. **Make the Whipped Cream Topping:**
   - In a chilled mixing bowl, whip the heavy cream until soft peaks form.
   - Add the powdered sugar and vanilla extract, and continue whipping until stiff peaks form.

6. **Serve:**
   - Spread or pipe the whipped cream over the chilled pie.
   - Garnish with additional lime zest or slices if desired.

Tips:

- If you can't find key limes, you can use regular limes for a similar flavor.
- To easily zest the limes, use a microplane grater or fine cheese grater.
- For a more intense lime flavor, you can add a few drops of lime extract to the filling.

Enjoy this tangy and creamy Key Lime Pie, a classic dessert that's sure to impress!

Fig Newtons

Ingredients:

For the Dough:

- 1 cup unsalted butter, softened
- 3/4 cup granulated sugar
- 1 large egg
- 1 teaspoon vanilla extract
- 2 cups all-purpose flour
- 1/4 teaspoon salt
- 1/2 teaspoon baking powder

For the Fig Filling:

- 1 1/2 cups dried figs, stems removed and chopped
- 1/4 cup honey or maple syrup
- 1/4 cup water
- Zest of 1 lemon (optional)
- 1/2 teaspoon ground cinnamon (optional)

Instructions:

1. **Prepare the Fig Filling:**
   - In a small saucepan, combine the chopped figs, honey or maple syrup, water, lemon zest (if using), and ground cinnamon (if using). Bring to a simmer over medium heat.
   - Reduce the heat to low and simmer for about 10-15 minutes, stirring occasionally, until the figs are soft and the mixture thickens.
   - Remove from heat and let the fig mixture cool slightly. Transfer to a food processor and pulse until smooth. Set aside to cool completely.
2. **Make the Dough:**
   - In a large mixing bowl, cream together the softened butter and granulated sugar until light and fluffy.
   - Add the egg and vanilla extract, mixing until well combined.
   - In a separate bowl, whisk together the flour, salt, and baking powder.
   - Gradually add the dry ingredients to the butter mixture, mixing until a dough forms.
3. **Assemble the Fig Newtons:**

- Divide the dough into two equal portions. Shape each portion into a rectangle and wrap each in plastic wrap. Chill in the refrigerator for at least 1 hour, or until firm.
4. **Roll Out the Dough:**
    - Preheat your oven to 350°F (175°C). Line a baking sheet with parchment paper.
    - On a lightly floured surface, roll out one portion of the chilled dough into a 10x12-inch rectangle, about 1/4 inch thick.
5. **Fill and Shape the Cookies:**
    - Spread half of the fig filling evenly over the rolled-out dough, leaving a small border around the edges.
    - Carefully fold one side of the dough over the filling to cover it, then fold the other side over to encase the filling completely. Press gently to seal the edges.
    - Transfer the filled dough to the prepared baking sheet. Repeat with the remaining dough and fig filling.
6. **Bake the Fig Newtons:**
    - Bake in the preheated oven for 20-25 minutes, or until the edges are lightly golden.
    - Remove from the oven and let the cookies cool on the baking sheet for 10 minutes.
    - Transfer to a wire rack to cool completely.
7. **Slice and Serve:**
    - Once cooled, slice the cookies into 1-inch wide bars.
    - Store the Fig Newtons in an airtight container at room temperature for up to 1 week.

Tips:

- You can adjust the sweetness of the fig filling by adding more or less honey or maple syrup.
- If the fig filling is too thick after processing, you can stir in a tablespoon of water at a time until it reaches your desired consistency.
- Feel free to add nuts or spices like cloves or nutmeg to the fig filling for added flavor.

Enjoy these homemade Fig Newtons with a cup of tea or as a snack any time of day!

Peanut Butter Cookies

Ingredients:

- 1/2 cup (1 stick) unsalted butter, softened
- 1/2 cup granulated sugar
- 1/2 cup packed light brown sugar
- 1/2 cup creamy peanut butter
- 1 large egg
- 1 teaspoon vanilla extract
- 1 1/4 cups all-purpose flour
- 1/2 teaspoon baking powder
- 1/2 teaspoon baking soda
- 1/4 teaspoon salt
- Additional granulated sugar (for rolling, optional)

Instructions:

1. **Preheat the Oven:**
   - Preheat your oven to 350°F (175°C). Line baking sheets with parchment paper or silicone baking mats.
2. **Cream Butter, Sugars, and Peanut Butter:**
   - In a large mixing bowl, cream together the softened butter, granulated sugar, and brown sugar until light and fluffy.
   - Add the creamy peanut butter and continue mixing until well combined.
3. **Add Egg and Vanilla:**
   - Beat in the egg and vanilla extract until smooth and creamy.
4. **Mix Dry Ingredients:**
   - In a separate bowl, whisk together the flour, baking powder, baking soda, and salt.
5. **Combine Wet and Dry Ingredients:**
   - Gradually add the dry ingredients to the wet ingredients, mixing until just combined. Be careful not to overmix.
6. **Form Cookie Dough Balls:**
   - Roll tablespoon-sized portions of dough into balls and place them on the prepared baking sheets, spacing them about 2 inches apart.
   - If desired, gently roll each ball in additional granulated sugar to coat lightly.
7. **Flatten with a Fork (Optional):**

- Using a fork, press down on each cookie ball to create a crisscross pattern on top.
8. **Bake the Cookies:**
   - Bake in the preheated oven for 10-12 minutes, or until the edges are lightly golden brown.
   - Remove from the oven and let the cookies cool on the baking sheets for 5 minutes before transferring them to a wire rack to cool completely.
9. **Cool and Enjoy:**
   - Allow the cookies to cool completely before serving. Store any leftovers in an airtight container at room temperature.

Tips:

- For chunky peanut butter cookies, use chunky peanut butter instead of creamy.
- If you prefer a softer cookie, slightly underbake them and let them cool on the baking sheet for a few minutes longer.
- These cookies are great for making ahead and freezing. Simply place the cooled cookies in a freezer-safe container or bag and freeze for up to 3 months.

Enjoy these classic Peanut Butter Cookies with a glass of milk or on their own for a delicious treat any time of day!

Watermelon Granita

Ingredients:

- 4 cups cubed seedless watermelon
- 1/2 cup granulated sugar (adjust according to sweetness of watermelon)
- Juice of 1 lime (optional, for added tang)
- Fresh mint leaves, for garnish (optional)

Instructions:

1. **Prepare the Watermelon:**
    - Cut the watermelon into cubes, removing any seeds if necessary.
2. **Blend the Watermelon:**
    - In a blender or food processor, blend the cubed watermelon until smooth.
3. **Add Sugar and Lime Juice:**
    - Add the granulated sugar and lime juice (if using) to the blended watermelon. Blend again until the sugar is dissolved and well combined.
4. **Pour into a Pan:**
    - Pour the watermelon mixture into a shallow, freezer-safe container or baking dish.
5. **Freeze the Granita:**
    - Place the container in the freezer and let it freeze for about 1 hour.
6. **Scrape and Stir:**
    - After 1 hour, use a fork to scrape and stir the mixture to break up any ice crystals that have formed. Pay special attention to the edges of the container.
7. **Continue Freezing and Scraping:**
    - Return the container to the freezer and repeat the scraping and stirring process every 30 minutes for 2-3 hours, or until the mixture is completely frozen and has a fluffy, granular texture.
8. **Serve:**
    - Once the Watermelon Granita is fully frozen and fluffy, scoop it into serving bowls or glasses.
    - Garnish with fresh mint leaves if desired.
9. **Enjoy:**
    - Serve immediately and enjoy this refreshing Watermelon Granita on a hot day!

Tips:

- For a more intense watermelon flavor, you can reduce the amount of sugar or omit it entirely, depending on the sweetness of your watermelon.
- Customize your granita by adding other fruits such as strawberries or mint leaves for added freshness.
- If you prefer a smoother texture, blend the mixture a bit longer before freezing.

Watermelon Granita is a simple yet delightful dessert that's sure to cool you down and satisfy your sweet cravings during the summer months.

Orange Chocolate Truffles

Ingredients:

- 8 ounces (about 1 1/3 cups) semi-sweet or dark chocolate, finely chopped
- 1/2 cup heavy cream
- Zest of 1 orange
- 2 tablespoons orange juice
- 1 tablespoon unsalted butter, softened
- Cocoa powder or powdered sugar, for rolling (optional)

Instructions:

1. **Prepare the Chocolate:**
    - Place the finely chopped chocolate in a heatproof bowl.
2. **Heat the Cream:**
    - In a small saucepan, heat the heavy cream over medium heat until it just begins to simmer. Do not let it boil.
3. **Combine with Chocolate:**
    - Pour the hot cream over the chopped chocolate. Let it sit for 1-2 minutes to soften the chocolate.
    - Gently stir the mixture with a spatula or whisk until the chocolate is completely melted and smooth.
4. **Add Orange Flavor:**
    - Stir in the orange zest, orange juice, and softened butter until well combined. The mixture will be smooth and glossy.
5. **Chill the Ganache:**
    - Cover the bowl with plastic wrap, pressing it directly onto the surface of the chocolate mixture to prevent a skin from forming.
    - Chill in the refrigerator for at least 2 hours, or until the ganache is firm enough to scoop and roll into balls.
6. **Shape the Truffles:**
    - Once chilled, use a spoon or a small cookie scoop to portion out the ganache.
    - Roll each portion into smooth balls using your hands. If the ganache is too soft, briefly refrigerate it until firm enough to handle.
7. **Coat the Truffles (Optional):**
    - Roll the truffles in cocoa powder, powdered sugar, or dip them in melted chocolate for a chocolate coating. This step is optional but adds a nice finish and extra flavor.

8. **Chill Again (Optional):**
   - If coated, place the truffles on a parchment-lined baking sheet and refrigerate for about 15-20 minutes to set the coating.
9. **Serve or Store:**
   - Serve the Orange Chocolate Truffles at room temperature. Store any leftovers in an airtight container in the refrigerator for up to 1 week.

Tips:

- For a stronger orange flavor, you can increase the amount of orange zest or juice.
- If the ganache becomes too firm to scoop, let it sit at room temperature for a few minutes to soften slightly.
- Experiment with different coatings like crushed nuts or shredded coconut for added texture and flavor variation.

These Orange Chocolate Truffles make for a luxurious and indulgent dessert or a thoughtful homemade gift for chocolate lovers. Enjoy the delicious combination of citrus and chocolate in every bite!

Pineapple Upside-Down Cake

Ingredients:

For the Topping:

- 1/4 cup unsalted butter
- 1/2 cup packed light brown sugar
- 1 can (20 ounces) pineapple slices, drained
- Maraschino cherries, drained (optional)

For the Cake Batter:

- 1 1/2 cups all-purpose flour
- 1 1/2 teaspoons baking powder
- 1/4 teaspoon salt
- 1/2 cup unsalted butter, softened
- 1 cup granulated sugar
- 2 large eggs
- 1 teaspoon vanilla extract
- 1/2 cup milk

Instructions:

1. **Preheat the Oven:**
   - Preheat your oven to 350°F (175°C). Grease a 9-inch round cake pan or a 9x9-inch square baking dish.
2. **Prepare the Topping:**
   - In a small saucepan, melt the butter over medium heat. Stir in the brown sugar until dissolved and smooth.
   - Pour the butter and sugar mixture into the prepared cake pan, spreading it evenly over the bottom.
   - Arrange the pineapple slices on top of the butter-sugar mixture. Place a maraschino cherry in the center of each pineapple slice and in between slices if desired.
3. **Make the Cake Batter:**
   - In a medium bowl, whisk together the flour, baking powder, and salt.
   - In a large mixing bowl, cream together the softened butter and granulated sugar until light and fluffy.
   - Beat in the eggs, one at a time, until well combined. Stir in the vanilla extract.

        - Gradually add the dry ingredients to the butter mixture alternately with the milk, beginning and ending with the dry ingredients. Mix until just combined.
 4. **Assemble and Bake:**
     - Pour the cake batter evenly over the pineapple slices in the prepared pan, spreading it carefully to cover the fruit.
 5. **Bake the Cake:**
     - Bake in the preheated oven for 40-45 minutes, or until a toothpick inserted into the center of the cake comes out clean.
 6. **Cool and Invert:**
     - Allow the cake to cool in the pan for about 10 minutes.
     - Place a serving plate or platter over the top of the cake pan and carefully invert the cake onto the plate. Let the pan rest on the cake for a few minutes to allow the topping to release.
 7. **Serve:**
     - Carefully lift off the cake pan. Slice and serve the Pineapple Upside-Down Cake warm or at room temperature.

Tips:

- For a richer flavor, you can add a splash of rum or pineapple juice to the butter-sugar mixture before pouring it into the cake pan.
- Ensure the cake pan is well-greased and the butter-sugar mixture is spread evenly to prevent sticking.
- Serve the cake with a dollop of whipped cream or a scoop of vanilla ice cream for a delightful treat.

Enjoy this classic Pineapple Upside-Down Cake with its caramelized pineapple topping and moist, buttery cake—it's sure to be a hit at any gathering!

Cinnamon Rolls

Ingredients:

For the Dough:

- 1 cup warm milk (about 110°F)
- 2 1/4 teaspoons (1 packet) active dry yeast
- 1/2 cup granulated sugar
- 1/3 cup unsalted butter, melted
- 2 large eggs
- 4 1/2 cups all-purpose flour
- 1 teaspoon salt

For the Filling:

- 1/2 cup unsalted butter, softened
- 1 cup packed brown sugar
- 2 tablespoons ground cinnamon

For the Cream Cheese Frosting:

- 4 ounces cream cheese, softened
- 1/4 cup unsalted butter, softened
- 1 cup powdered sugar
- 1/2 teaspoon vanilla extract
- Pinch of salt

Instructions:

1. **Activate the Yeast:**
   - In a small bowl, combine the warm milk and yeast. Let it sit for 5-10 minutes until foamy.
2. **Make the Dough:**
   - In a large mixing bowl or the bowl of a stand mixer fitted with a dough hook, combine the activated yeast mixture, sugar, melted butter, eggs, flour, and salt.
   - Mix on low speed until the dough begins to come together.
   - Increase the speed to medium and knead the dough for about 5-7 minutes until it is smooth and elastic. If kneading by hand, knead on a lightly floured surface for about 8-10 minutes.

3. **First Rise:**
   - Place the dough in a greased bowl, cover with a clean kitchen towel or plastic wrap, and let it rise in a warm place for about 1-1.5 hours, or until doubled in size.
4. **Prepare the Filling:**
   - In a small bowl, combine the softened butter, brown sugar, and ground cinnamon until well mixed.
5. **Roll Out the Dough:**
   - Punch down the risen dough and transfer it to a lightly floured surface.
   - Roll out the dough into a rectangle about 16x20 inches in size.
6. **Fill and Roll:**
   - Spread the cinnamon-sugar filling evenly over the rolled-out dough, leaving a small border around the edges.
   - Starting from one long edge, tightly roll up the dough into a log.
   - Cut the log into 12 even slices using a sharp knife or dental floss for clean cuts.
7. **Second Rise:**
   - Place the rolls in a greased 9x13-inch baking pan or two 9-inch round pans, leaving a little space between each roll.
   - Cover the pan(s) with a kitchen towel and let the rolls rise for another 30-45 minutes, until they are puffy and have doubled in size.
8. **Bake the Rolls:**
   - Preheat your oven to 350°F (175°C).
   - Bake the cinnamon rolls in the preheated oven for 20-25 minutes, or until golden brown.
9. **Make the Cream Cheese Frosting:**
   - While the rolls are baking, prepare the cream cheese frosting. In a medium bowl, beat together the softened cream cheese and butter until smooth and creamy.
   - Add the powdered sugar, vanilla extract, and a pinch of salt. Beat until smooth and creamy.
10. **Frost the Rolls:**
    - Remove the cinnamon rolls from the oven and let them cool slightly.
    - Spread the cream cheese frosting evenly over the warm rolls.
11. **Serve:**
    - Serve the cinnamon rolls warm. Enjoy their gooey centers and sweet cinnamon flavor!

Tips:

- For an overnight option, after shaping the rolls and placing them in the baking pan, cover tightly with plastic wrap and refrigerate overnight. In the morning, let them come to room temperature and rise for about 1 hour before baking.
- You can add chopped nuts or raisins to the filling for extra texture and flavor.
- Store leftover cinnamon rolls in an airtight container at room temperature for up to 2 days, or in the refrigerator for up to 5 days. Warm them in the microwave before serving.

These homemade Cinnamon Rolls are sure to become a favorite treat for breakfast or any time you crave a deliciously sweet indulgence!

Chia Seed Pudding

Ingredients:

- 1/4 cup chia seeds
- 1 cup milk (dairy or plant-based such as almond milk, coconut milk, etc.)
- 1-2 tablespoons maple syrup or honey (adjust to taste)
- 1/2 teaspoon vanilla extract
- Optional toppings: fresh berries, sliced fruits, nuts, shredded coconut, chocolate chips, etc.

Instructions:

1. **Combine Ingredients:**
    - In a bowl or jar, mix together the chia seeds, milk, maple syrup (or honey), and vanilla extract. Stir well to combine.
2. **Let it Set:**
    - Cover the bowl or jar and refrigerate for at least 2 hours, or preferably overnight. This allows the chia seeds to absorb the liquid and thicken to a pudding-like consistency.
3. **Stir Occasionally:**
    - After the first hour, stir the mixture again to break up any clumps and ensure the chia seeds are evenly distributed.
4. **Serve:**
    - Once the pudding has reached the desired consistency (thick and creamy), give it a final stir.
    - Spoon the Chia Seed Pudding into serving bowls or jars.
5. **Add Toppings:**
    - Garnish with your favorite toppings such as fresh berries, sliced fruits, nuts, shredded coconut, or chocolate chips.
6. **Enjoy:**
    - Serve the Chia Seed Pudding chilled and enjoy it as a nutritious and satisfying meal or snack!

Tips:

- Experiment with different flavors by adding cocoa powder, matcha powder, or cinnamon to the pudding mixture before refrigerating.
- Adjust the sweetness level to your preference by varying the amount of maple syrup or honey.

- Chia Seed Pudding can be stored in the refrigerator for up to 5 days. Keep it covered to maintain freshness.

This Chia Seed Pudding recipe is versatile, delicious, and packed with fiber, omega-3 fatty acids, and antioxidants, making it a healthy addition to your diet. Customize it with your favorite toppings and flavors for a delightful treat any time of day!

Pistachio Ice Cream

Ingredients:

- 1 cup shelled pistachios, unsalted
- 1 1/2 cups whole milk
- 1 cup heavy cream
- 2/3 cup granulated sugar
- 4 large egg yolks
- 1 teaspoon vanilla extract
- 1/4 teaspoon almond extract (optional, for extra flavor)
- A pinch of salt

Instructions:

1. **Prepare the Pistachios:**
   - In a food processor or blender, pulse the pistachios until finely ground. Be careful not to over-process into a paste; you want a fine grind with some texture.
2. **Infuse the Milk and Cream:**
   - In a medium saucepan, combine the ground pistachios, whole milk, and heavy cream. Heat over medium heat until it just begins to simmer. Remove from heat, cover, and let steep for about 1 hour to infuse the flavors.
3. **Strain the Mixture:**
   - After steeping, strain the milk and cream mixture through a fine-mesh sieve into a clean saucepan, pressing on the pistachios to extract as much flavor as possible. Discard the ground pistachios.
4. **Prepare the Ice Cream Base:**
   - In a separate bowl, whisk together the sugar, egg yolks, vanilla extract, almond extract (if using), and salt until well combined.
5. **Temper the Eggs:**
   - Gradually whisk a small amount of the warm milk mixture into the egg yolk mixture to temper the eggs. This prevents them from curdling.
6. **Cook the Custard:**
   - Gradually whisk the tempered egg mixture back into the saucepan with the remaining milk mixture. Cook over medium heat, stirring constantly with a wooden spoon or spatula, until the custard thickens and coats the back of the spoon. This should take about 5-7 minutes. Do not let it boil.
7. **Chill the Custard:**

- Remove the custard from heat and immediately strain it through a fine-mesh sieve into a clean bowl. This removes any bits of cooked egg and ensures a smooth texture.
- Place plastic wrap directly on the surface of the custard to prevent a skin from forming. Chill in the refrigerator for at least 4 hours or overnight until thoroughly chilled.

8. **Churn the Ice Cream:**
   - Once chilled, pour the custard into an ice cream maker and churn according to the manufacturer's instructions until it reaches a soft-serve consistency.
9. **Freeze the Ice Cream:**
   - Transfer the churned ice cream into a freezer-safe container. Press a piece of parchment paper or plastic wrap directly on the surface of the ice cream to prevent ice crystals from forming. Cover with a lid and freeze for at least 4 hours, or until firm.
10. **Serve:**
    - Scoop the Pistachio Ice Cream into bowls or cones and enjoy its creamy texture and rich pistachio flavor!

Tips:

- For an extra pop of color, add a few drops of green food coloring to the custard mixture before churning.
- Garnish with chopped pistachios or a drizzle of melted chocolate for added indulgence.
- Store leftover Pistachio Ice Cream in the freezer for up to 2 weeks. Allow it to soften slightly at room temperature before serving.

Homemade Pistachio Ice Cream is a luxurious treat with its delicate nutty flavor and creamy texture. Enjoy this delicious dessert on its own or alongside your favorite desserts for a delightful ending to any meal!

Cranberry Orange Scones

Ingredients:

- 2 cups all-purpose flour
- 1/4 cup granulated sugar
- 1 tablespoon baking powder
- 1/2 teaspoon salt
- Zest of 1 orange
- 1/2 cup unsalted butter, cold and cut into small cubes
- 1/2 cup dried cranberries
- 1/2 cup milk (plus extra for brushing)
- 1 large egg
- 1 teaspoon vanilla extract

For the Glaze (optional):

- 1 cup powdered sugar
- 2-3 tablespoons freshly squeezed orange juice
- Zest of 1 orange (optional)

Instructions:

1. **Preheat the Oven:**
   - Preheat your oven to 400°F (200°C). Line a baking sheet with parchment paper or silicone mat.
2. **Mix Dry Ingredients:**
   - In a large bowl, whisk together the flour, sugar, baking powder, salt, and orange zest.
3. **Cut in Butter:**
   - Add the cold butter cubes to the dry ingredients. Use a pastry cutter, fork, or your fingertips to cut the butter into the flour mixture until it resembles coarse crumbs.
4. **Add Cranberries:**
   - Stir in the dried cranberries until evenly distributed in the flour mixture.
5. **Combine Wet Ingredients:**
   - In a separate bowl, whisk together the milk, egg, and vanilla extract.
6. **Form Dough:**

- Pour the wet ingredients into the dry ingredients. Stir gently with a wooden spoon or spatula until just combined. Be careful not to overmix; the dough should be shaggy.

7. **Shape Scones:**
   - Transfer the dough onto a lightly floured surface. Pat the dough into a circle about 1 inch thick.
   - Using a sharp knife or bench scraper, cut the circle into 8 wedges.
8. **Bake Scones:**
   - Place the scones on the prepared baking sheet, spacing them a few inches apart.
   - Brush the tops of the scones lightly with milk.
9. **Bake:**
   - Bake in the preheated oven for 15-18 minutes, or until the scones are golden brown on top and cooked through.
10. **Make Glaze (optional):**
    - While the scones are baking, prepare the glaze. In a small bowl, whisk together the powdered sugar, orange juice, and orange zest until smooth. Adjust the consistency with more juice or sugar as needed.
11. **Cool and Glaze:**
    - Remove the scones from the oven and let them cool on a wire rack for a few minutes.
    - Drizzle the glaze over the warm scones, allowing it to set for a few minutes before serving.
12. **Serve:**
    - Enjoy the Cranberry Orange Scones warm or at room temperature with a hot cup of tea or coffee!

Tips:

- For extra flaky scones, handle the dough as little as possible and keep the butter cold.
- You can substitute fresh cranberries for dried ones, adjusting the sweetness as needed.
- Store leftover scones in an airtight container at room temperature for up to 3 days. Warm briefly in the oven before serving.

These Cranberry Orange Scones are bursting with fruity flavors and are sure to be a hit at your breakfast table or brunch gathering. Enjoy the tender texture and zesty orange notes in every bite!

Strawberry Shortcake

Ingredients:

For the Biscuits:

- 2 cups all-purpose flour
- 1/4 cup granulated sugar
- 1 tablespoon baking powder
- 1/2 teaspoon salt
- 1/2 cup unsalted butter, cold and cut into small cubes
- 3/4 cup buttermilk (or milk with 1 tablespoon of vinegar or lemon juice)
- 1 teaspoon vanilla extract
- 1 tablespoon heavy cream or milk, for brushing

For the Strawberries:

- 1 pound fresh strawberries, hulled and sliced
- 2-3 tablespoons granulated sugar (adjust to taste)
- 1 teaspoon vanilla extract

For the Whipped Cream:

- 1 cup heavy cream, chilled
- 2 tablespoons powdered sugar
- 1 teaspoon vanilla extract

Instructions:

1. **Preheat the Oven:**
   - Preheat your oven to 400°F (200°C). Line a baking sheet with parchment paper or silicone mat.
2. **Prepare the Biscuits:**
   - In a large bowl, whisk together the flour, sugar, baking powder, and salt.
   - Cut in the cold butter using a pastry cutter, fork, or your fingertips until the mixture resembles coarse crumbs.
3. **Mix Wet Ingredients:**
   - In a separate bowl, combine the buttermilk and vanilla extract.
4. **Combine and Form Dough:**

- Pour the wet ingredients into the dry ingredients and stir with a wooden spoon or spatula until just combined. Be careful not to overmix; the dough should be shaggy.
5. **Shape Biscuits:**
    - Transfer the dough onto a lightly floured surface. Pat the dough into a rectangle about 1 inch thick.
    - Use a biscuit cutter or a glass with a diameter of about 2.5 inches to cut out biscuits. Place them on the prepared baking sheet, reshaping the dough as needed. You should get about 6-8 biscuits.
6. **Brush and Bake:**
    - Brush the tops of the biscuits with heavy cream or milk.
    - Bake in the preheated oven for 15-18 minutes, or until the biscuits are golden brown on top. Remove from the oven and let cool slightly on a wire rack.
7. **Prepare the Strawberries:**
    - In a bowl, gently toss the sliced strawberries with sugar and vanilla extract. Let them sit for about 15-20 minutes to macerate and release their juices.
8. **Make the Whipped Cream:**
    - In a chilled bowl, whip the heavy cream, powdered sugar, and vanilla extract until soft peaks form. Be careful not to overwhip.
9. **Assemble the Shortcakes:**
    - Slice each biscuit in half horizontally using a serrated knife.
    - Spoon a generous amount of macerated strawberries and their juices onto the bottom half of each biscuit.
    - Top with a dollop of whipped cream.
    - Place the top half of the biscuit over the whipped cream.
10. **Serve:**
    - Serve the Strawberry Shortcakes immediately, garnished with extra whipped cream and strawberries if desired.

Tips:

- You can customize the sweetness of the biscuits by adjusting the amount of sugar in the dough.
- For a shortcut, you can use store-bought biscuits or pound cake instead of making the biscuits from scratch.
- Leftover biscuits can be stored in an airtight container at room temperature for up to 2 days. Reheat briefly in the oven before serving.

Enjoy these homemade Strawberry Shortcakes with their buttery biscuits, juicy strawberries, and fluffy whipped cream—a perfect dessert for spring and summer gatherings!

Date Balls

Ingredients:

- 1 cup Medjool dates, pitted (about 10-12 dates)
- 1 cup nuts (such as almonds, walnuts, or pecans)
- 2 tablespoons cocoa powder (optional, for chocolate flavor)
- 1 tablespoon coconut oil (optional, for binding)
- Pinch of salt
- Optional coatings: shredded coconut, cocoa powder, chopped nuts, sesame seeds, etc.

Instructions:

1. **Prepare the Dates:**
    - If the dates are not already pitted, remove the pits. Place the dates in a food processor.
2. **Add Nuts and Flavorings:**
    - Add the nuts, cocoa powder (if using), coconut oil (if using), and a pinch of salt to the food processor with the dates.
3. **Blend Until Combined:**
    - Process the mixture until it forms a sticky dough-like consistency. The nuts should be finely chopped, and the mixture should easily hold together when pressed between your fingers.
4. **Form Balls:**
    - Scoop out small portions of the mixture and roll them between your palms to form balls. If the mixture is too sticky to handle, you can wet your hands slightly with water.
5. **Coat (Optional):**
    - Roll the date balls in shredded coconut, cocoa powder, chopped nuts, sesame seeds, or any other coating of your choice to add texture and flavor.
6. **Chill (Optional):**
    - For firmer date balls, place them in the refrigerator for about 30 minutes to set.
7. **Store and Serve:**
    - Store the date balls in an airtight container in the refrigerator for up to 2 weeks. They can also be frozen for longer storage.
    - Serve chilled or at room temperature as a healthy snack or dessert.

Tips:

- Experiment with different nuts and flavorings to customize your date balls. For example, you can add vanilla extract, cinnamon, or even citrus zest for additional flavor.
- Adjust the sweetness by adding more dates or a touch of honey or maple syrup if desired.
- Date balls are naturally gluten-free and vegan, making them suitable for various dietary preferences.

These homemade date balls are not only delicious but also packed with fiber, vitamins, and minerals from the dates and nuts. Enjoy them guilt-free as a quick energy boost or a satisfying sweet treat!

Blackberry Crumble

Ingredients:

For the Filling:

- 4 cups fresh blackberries (or frozen, thawed)
- 1/3 cup granulated sugar (adjust according to sweetness of berries)
- 1 tablespoon cornstarch
- 1 tablespoon lemon juice
- Zest of 1 lemon (optional)

For the Crumble Topping:

- 1 cup old-fashioned rolled oats
- 1/2 cup all-purpose flour
- 1/2 cup brown sugar
- 1/2 teaspoon ground cinnamon
- 1/4 teaspoon salt
- 1/2 cup unsalted butter, cold and cut into small cubes

Instructions:

1. **Preheat the Oven:**
   - Preheat your oven to 350°F (175°C). Grease a 9-inch baking dish or individual ramekins.
2. **Prepare the Filling:**
   - In a large bowl, gently toss the blackberries with sugar, cornstarch, lemon juice, and lemon zest (if using) until well combined. Transfer the blackberry mixture to the prepared baking dish or ramekins.
3. **Make the Crumble Topping:**
   - In another bowl, combine the rolled oats, flour, brown sugar, cinnamon, and salt. Mix well.
   - Add the cold cubed butter to the oat mixture. Use your fingers or a pastry cutter to cut the butter into the dry ingredients until it resembles coarse crumbs with some pea-sized pieces of butter.
4. **Assemble and Bake:**
   - Sprinkle the crumble topping evenly over the blackberry filling in the baking dish or ramekins.

        - Place the baking dish on a baking sheet (to catch any drips) and bake in the preheated oven for 35-40 minutes, or until the topping is golden brown and the filling is bubbly.
5. **Cool and Serve:**
        - Remove the blackberry crumble from the oven and let it cool for 10-15 minutes before serving.
        - Serve warm with a scoop of vanilla ice cream or a dollop of whipped cream, if desired.

Tips:

- You can substitute blackberries with other berries such as raspberries, blueberries, or a combination of berries.
- Adjust the sweetness of the filling according to your taste and the natural sweetness of the berries.
- Store leftover blackberry crumble covered in the refrigerator for up to 3 days. Reheat gently in the oven before serving.

This blackberry crumble is a comforting and versatile dessert that highlights the natural sweetness of blackberries with a crunchy oat topping. Enjoy it as a cozy treat for family gatherings or special occasions!

Pecan Pie Bars

Ingredients:

For the Crust:

- 1 1/2 cups all-purpose flour
- 1/2 cup powdered sugar
- 1/4 teaspoon salt
- 3/4 cup unsalted butter, cold and cut into small cubes

For the Filling:

- 3/4 cup unsalted butter
- 1 cup packed light brown sugar
- 1/2 cup honey or maple syrup
- 2 tablespoons heavy cream or milk
- 4 cups pecan halves

Instructions:

1. **Preheat the Oven and Prepare the Pan:**
    - Preheat your oven to 350°F (175°C). Grease a 9x13-inch baking dish or line it with parchment paper, leaving an overhang on the sides for easy removal.
2. **Make the Crust:**
    - In a medium bowl, whisk together the flour, powdered sugar, and salt.
    - Cut in the cold butter using a pastry cutter or your fingertips until the mixture resembles coarse crumbs and starts to come together.
    - Press the crust mixture evenly into the bottom of the prepared baking dish.
    - Bake the crust in the preheated oven for 15-18 minutes, or until lightly golden. Remove from the oven and set aside.
3. **Prepare the Filling:**
    - In a medium saucepan, melt the butter over medium heat.
    - Stir in the brown sugar, honey or maple syrup, and heavy cream or milk. Cook, stirring constantly, until the mixture comes to a simmer.
    - Remove the saucepan from the heat and stir in the pecan halves until they are evenly coated.
4. **Assemble and Bake:**
    - Pour the pecan filling evenly over the baked crust, spreading it out with a spatula if needed.

- Return the baking dish to the oven and bake for an additional 20-25 minutes, or until the filling is bubbling and golden brown.
5. **Cool and Serve:**
    - Allow the pecan pie bars to cool completely in the baking dish on a wire rack.
    - Once cooled, use the parchment paper overhang to lift the bars out of the baking dish. Transfer to a cutting board and slice into bars or squares.
6. **Store and Enjoy:**
    - Store leftover pecan pie bars in an airtight container at room temperature for up to 3 days, or in the refrigerator for up to a week.

Tips:

- For easier slicing, chill the bars in the refrigerator for about 1 hour before cutting into squares.
- You can customize the sweetness by adjusting the amount of sugar or honey/maple syrup in the filling.
- Serve pecan pie bars as a decadent dessert or treat during holiday gatherings, parties, or as a special snack with coffee or tea.

These pecan pie bars capture the essence of pecan pie in a convenient bar form, making them perfect for sharing and enjoying on various occasions. Enjoy the rich flavors of pecans and caramelized filling in every bite!

Oatmeal Raisin Cookies

Ingredients:

- 1 cup unsalted butter, softened
- 1 cup packed light brown sugar
- 1/2 cup granulated sugar
- 2 large eggs
- 1 teaspoon vanilla extract
- 1 1/2 cups all-purpose flour
- 1 teaspoon baking soda
- 1 teaspoon ground cinnamon
- 1/2 teaspoon salt
- 3 cups old-fashioned rolled oats
- 1 cup raisins (or chopped dates, dried cranberries, or a mix of dried fruits)
- Optional: 1/2 cup chopped nuts (such as walnuts or pecans)

Instructions:

1. **Preheat the Oven:**
   - Preheat your oven to 350°F (175°C). Line baking sheets with parchment paper or silicone baking mats.
2. **Cream Butter and Sugars:**
   - In a large bowl, cream together the softened butter, brown sugar, and granulated sugar until light and fluffy.
3. **Add Eggs and Vanilla:**
   - Beat in the eggs, one at a time, until well combined. Stir in the vanilla extract.
4. **Combine Dry Ingredients:**
   - In a separate bowl, whisk together the flour, baking soda, ground cinnamon, and salt.
5. **Mix Wet and Dry Ingredients:**
   - Gradually add the dry ingredients to the creamed butter mixture, mixing until just combined.
6. **Add Oats and Raisins:**
   - Stir in the rolled oats and raisins (and chopped nuts, if using) until evenly distributed in the dough.
7. **Shape Cookies:**
   - Drop tablespoon-sized scoops of dough onto the prepared baking sheets, spacing them about 2 inches apart.

- Optionally, you can lightly flatten each cookie with the back of a spoon or fork.
8. **Bake:**
    - Bake in the preheated oven for 10-12 minutes, or until the edges are golden brown and the tops are set.
9. **Cool and Serve:**
    - Allow the cookies to cool on the baking sheets for a few minutes before transferring them to a wire rack to cool completely.
10. **Store:**
    - Store oatmeal raisin cookies in an airtight container at room temperature for up to 1 week.

Tips:

- For chewier cookies, slightly underbake them; for crispier cookies, bake them a bit longer.
- You can customize these cookies by adding chocolate chips, shredded coconut, or other mix-ins of your choice.
- If you prefer softer raisins, soak them in warm water for 10 minutes, then drain well before adding to the cookie dough.

These oatmeal raisin cookies are perfect for snacking, sharing with friends, or enjoying with a glass of milk. Their hearty oatmeal texture and sweet raisins make them a timeless favorite!

Maple Walnut Fudge

Ingredients:

- 2 cups granulated sugar
- 1 cup packed light brown sugar
- 3/4 cup unsalted butter
- 2/3 cup evaporated milk
- 1 cup pure maple syrup
- 1 teaspoon vanilla extract
- 2 cups chopped walnuts
- 1 cup marshmallow creme or marshmallows (about 8 large marshmallows)
- Pinch of salt

Instructions:

1. **Prepare Pan:**
   - Line an 8x8-inch square baking dish with parchment paper, leaving an overhang on the sides for easy removal. Lightly grease the parchment paper with butter.
2. **Cook Fudge Mixture:**
   - In a large, heavy-bottomed saucepan, combine the granulated sugar, brown sugar, butter, evaporated milk, and maple syrup.
   - Stirring constantly, bring the mixture to a boil over medium heat. Once boiling, reduce the heat to medium-low and continue to cook, stirring frequently, until a candy thermometer reads 234°F (soft-ball stage). This typically takes about 10-15 minutes.
3. **Remove from Heat:**
   - Once the mixture reaches 234°F, remove the saucepan from the heat. Stir in the vanilla extract, chopped walnuts, marshmallow creme (or marshmallows), and a pinch of salt. Mix until everything is well combined and the marshmallows are fully melted.
4. **Pour and Cool:**
   - Immediately pour the hot fudge mixture into the prepared baking dish, spreading it evenly with a spatula.
5. **Let Set:**
   - Let the fudge cool at room temperature until completely set, which may take about 2 hours.
6. **Slice and Serve:**

- Once the fudge is completely cooled and set, lift it out of the baking dish using the parchment paper overhang. Place it on a cutting board and cut into squares with a sharp knife.
7. **Store:**
    - Store maple walnut fudge in an airtight container at room temperature for up to 1 week. For longer storage, keep it refrigerated for up to 2 weeks.

Tips:

- Use a candy thermometer to ensure the fudge reaches the soft-ball stage (234°F) for the best texture.
- Stir the fudge mixture gently and consistently to prevent it from scorching or sticking to the bottom of the pan.
- You can customize this fudge by adding other nuts like pecans or almonds, or by drizzling melted chocolate over the top once it's set.

Enjoy this indulgent maple walnut fudge as a sweet treat for holidays, parties, or whenever you crave a delightful combination of maple and nuts!

Cherry Almond Tart

Ingredients:

For the Crust:

- 1 1/4 cups all-purpose flour
- 1/4 cup granulated sugar
- 1/4 teaspoon salt
- 1/2 cup unsalted butter, cold and cut into small pieces
- 1 egg yolk
- 1 tablespoon ice water (if needed)

For the Almond Filling:

- 1 cup almond flour or finely ground almonds
- 1/2 cup granulated sugar
- 1/4 cup unsalted butter, softened
- 1 egg
- 1 teaspoon almond extract
- 1/4 teaspoon salt

For the Cherry Topping:

- 2 cups fresh cherries, pitted and halved (or use frozen cherries, thawed and drained)
- 1 tablespoon granulated sugar
- 1 tablespoon cornstarch

Optional Garnish:

- Sliced almonds
- Powdered sugar, for dusting

Instructions:

1. **Make the Crust:**
   - In a food processor, pulse together the flour, sugar, and salt until combined.
   - Add the cold butter and pulse until the mixture resembles coarse crumbs.
   - Add the egg yolk and pulse again until the dough comes together. If needed, add 1 tablespoon of ice water to help bind the dough.

    - Form the dough into a disk, wrap it in plastic wrap, and refrigerate for at least 30 minutes.
2. **Prepare the Almond Filling:**
    - In a medium bowl, cream together the almond flour (or ground almonds), sugar, softened butter, egg, almond extract, and salt until smooth and well combined. Set aside.
3. **Preheat the Oven:**
    - Preheat your oven to 350°F (175°C). Grease a 9-inch tart pan with a removable bottom.
4. **Roll Out the Dough:**
    - On a lightly floured surface, roll out the chilled dough into a circle about 12 inches in diameter. Carefully transfer the dough to the prepared tart pan, pressing it into the bottom and up the sides. Trim off any excess dough.
5. **Assemble the Tart:**
    - Spread the almond filling evenly over the bottom of the tart crust.
6. **Prepare the Cherry Topping:**
    - In a bowl, toss the halved cherries with sugar and cornstarch until well coated.
    - Arrange the cherries over the almond filling in a decorative pattern.
7. **Bake the Tart:**
    - Place the tart on a baking sheet (to catch any drips) and bake in the preheated oven for 35-40 minutes, or until the crust is golden brown and the cherries are bubbling.
8. **Cool and Serve:**
    - Allow the cherry almond tart to cool in the tart pan for 10-15 minutes before carefully removing it from the pan and transferring it to a wire rack to cool completely.
    - Optionally, garnish with sliced almonds and dust with powdered sugar before serving.
9. **Serve and Enjoy:**
    - Slice the cherry almond tart and serve it at room temperature. Enjoy this delicious dessert on its own or with a dollop of whipped cream or a scoop of vanilla ice cream.

Tips:

- If using frozen cherries, make sure to thaw them completely and drain any excess liquid before using.

- Feel free to experiment with other fruits such as raspberries or blueberries for different variations of this tart.
- Store any leftover tart in an airtight container in the refrigerator for up to 3 days.

This cherry almond tart is perfect for showcasing fresh cherries during their peak season or as a delightful treat for special occasions. Enjoy the combination of tender almond filling and juicy cherries in every bite!

Lemon Poppy Seed Cake

Ingredients:

For the Cake:

- 1 1/2 cups all-purpose flour
- 2 tablespoons poppy seeds
- 1 teaspoon baking powder
- 1/2 teaspoon baking soda
- 1/4 teaspoon salt
- 1/2 cup unsalted butter, softened
- 1 cup granulated sugar
- 2 large eggs
- 1 tablespoon lemon zest (from about 2 lemons)
- 1/4 cup fresh lemon juice
- 1/2 cup buttermilk (or substitute with 1/2 cup milk mixed with 1/2 tablespoon lemon juice or vinegar)

For the Glaze:

- 1 cup powdered sugar
- 2-3 tablespoons fresh lemon juice

Instructions:

1. **Preheat the Oven:**
   - Preheat your oven to 350°F (175°C). Grease and flour a 9x5-inch loaf pan or line it with parchment paper for easy removal.
2. **Prepare Dry Ingredients:**
   - In a medium bowl, whisk together the flour, poppy seeds, baking powder, baking soda, and salt. Set aside.
3. **Cream Butter and Sugar:**
   - In a large bowl, cream together the softened butter and granulated sugar until light and fluffy.
4. **Add Eggs and Lemon Zest:**
   - Beat in the eggs, one at a time, until well combined. Stir in the lemon zest.
5. **Combine Wet and Dry Ingredients:**
   - Gradually add the dry flour mixture to the creamed butter mixture, alternating with additions of the buttermilk and lemon juice. Begin and end with the dry ingredients, mixing until just combined. Do not overmix.

6. **Bake the Cake:**
   - Pour the batter into the prepared loaf pan and spread it evenly with a spatula.
   - Bake in the preheated oven for 45-55 minutes, or until a toothpick inserted into the center comes out clean or with a few moist crumbs.
7. **Cool the Cake:**
   - Allow the cake to cool in the pan for about 10 minutes, then remove it from the pan and transfer it to a wire rack to cool completely.
8. **Prepare the Glaze:**
   - In a small bowl, whisk together the powdered sugar and enough fresh lemon juice to create a smooth glaze consistency.
9. **Glaze the Cake:**
   - Once the cake has cooled, drizzle the lemon glaze over the top. Allow the glaze to set before slicing and serving.

Tips:

- For a more intense lemon flavor, increase the amount of lemon zest and juice used in the cake batter.
- Ensure all ingredients are at room temperature before beginning to ensure even mixing and a smooth batter.
- Store leftovers in an airtight container at room temperature for up to 3 days, or in the refrigerator for longer freshness.

Enjoy this lemon poppy seed cake as a delightful dessert or a sweet treat with a cup of tea or coffee. Its bright lemony flavor and delicate poppy seed crunch make it a favorite for any occasion!

Coconut Rice Pudding

Ingredients:

- 1 cup jasmine rice (or any medium-grain rice)
- 2 cups water
- 1 can (13.5 oz) coconut milk (full-fat for creamier pudding)
- 1 can (14 oz) sweetened condensed milk
- 1 cup coconut cream (optional, for extra coconut flavor)
- 1 teaspoon vanilla extract
- 1/4 teaspoon salt
- 1/2 cup shredded coconut (sweetened or unsweetened), toasted (optional, for garnish)
- Fresh berries or mango slices, for garnish (optional)

Instructions:

1. **Cook the Rice:**
   - Rinse the jasmine rice under cold water until the water runs clear.
   - In a medium saucepan, combine the rinsed rice and 2 cups of water. Bring to a boil over medium-high heat.
   - Reduce the heat to low, cover, and simmer for about 15-20 minutes, or until the rice is tender and has absorbed most of the water.
2. **Prepare the Pudding:**
   - Once the rice is cooked, stir in the coconut milk, sweetened condensed milk, coconut cream (if using), vanilla extract, and salt.
   - Bring the mixture to a gentle simmer over medium heat, stirring frequently to prevent sticking or burning on the bottom of the pan.
3. **Simmer and Thicken:**
   - Reduce the heat to low and simmer the rice pudding, uncovered, stirring occasionally, for about 20-25 minutes or until the mixture thickens to a creamy consistency. The rice should be soft and the pudding should coat the back of a spoon.
4. **Cool and Serve:**
   - Remove the rice pudding from the heat and let it cool slightly.
   - Serve warm, at room temperature, or chilled. Garnish with toasted shredded coconut and fresh berries or mango slices if desired.
5. **Store:**
   - Store leftover coconut rice pudding in an airtight container in the refrigerator for up to 3 days. Serve chilled or gently reheat before serving.

Tips:

- For a richer pudding, you can use coconut cream in addition to coconut milk.
- Adjust the sweetness by adding more or less sweetened condensed milk to suit your taste.
- Stir the pudding frequently while simmering to ensure even cooking and to prevent sticking.

This coconut rice pudding is a delightful dessert that brings together the tropical flavors of coconut with the comforting creaminess of rice pudding. Enjoy it as a satisfying treat any time of the day!

Espresso Brownies

Ingredients:

- 1/2 cup unsalted butter
- 1 cup granulated sugar
- 2 large eggs
- 1 teaspoon vanilla extract
- 1/4 cup brewed espresso or strong coffee, cooled
- 1/2 cup all-purpose flour
- 1/3 cup unsweetened cocoa powder
- 1/4 teaspoon salt
- 1/2 cup semi-sweet chocolate chips or chunks

Instructions:

1. **Preheat the Oven and Prepare Pan:**
    - Preheat your oven to 350°F (175°C). Grease and line an 8x8-inch baking pan with parchment paper, leaving an overhang on the sides for easy removal.
2. **Melt Butter:**
    - In a medium saucepan, melt the butter over medium heat. Stir occasionally until fully melted and smooth. Remove from heat and let it cool slightly.
3. **Mix Wet Ingredients:**
    - In a large bowl, whisk together the granulated sugar, eggs, and vanilla extract until well combined.
4. **Add Espresso:**
    - Stir in the cooled brewed espresso or strong coffee into the sugar and egg mixture.
5. **Combine Dry Ingredients:**
    - In another bowl, sift together the flour, cocoa powder, and salt.
6. **Combine Wet and Dry Ingredients:**
    - Gradually add the dry ingredients to the wet ingredients, mixing until just combined. Do not overmix.
7. **Add Chocolate Chips:**
    - Fold in the chocolate chips or chunks until evenly distributed in the batter.
8. **Bake:**
    - Pour the batter into the prepared baking pan and spread it evenly with a spatula.

- Bake in the preheated oven for 25-30 minutes, or until a toothpick inserted into the center comes out with a few moist crumbs.
9. **Cool and Serve:**
    - Allow the brownies to cool completely in the pan on a wire rack before cutting into squares.
10. **Optional: Dust with Cocoa Powder:**
    - Dust the top of the brownies with cocoa powder before serving, if desired.

Tips:

- For a stronger espresso flavor, add 1-2 tablespoons of instant espresso powder to the batter.
- Do not overbake the brownies to ensure they stay moist and fudgy.
- Store leftover brownies in an airtight container at room temperature for up to 3 days, or refrigerate for longer freshness.

These espresso brownies are perfect for indulging in a rich chocolatey treat with a subtle coffee kick. Enjoy them with a cup of coffee or as a delightful dessert after any meal!

Salted Caramel Pretzel Bark

Ingredients:

- 2 cups mini pretzels (or pretzel twists), broken into pieces
- 1 cup unsalted butter
- 1 cup packed light brown sugar
- 1/2 teaspoon vanilla extract
- 2 cups semi-sweet chocolate chips
- Sea salt flakes, for sprinkling

Instructions:

1. **Prepare Baking Sheet:**
    - Line a large baking sheet with parchment paper or a silicone baking mat. Arrange the pretzel pieces evenly on the prepared baking sheet.
2. **Make Caramel:**
    - In a medium saucepan, melt the butter over medium heat. Stir in the brown sugar and cook, stirring constantly, until the mixture comes to a boil. Boil for 2-3 minutes without stirring.
3. **Add Vanilla Extract:**
    - Remove the saucepan from heat and stir in the vanilla extract. Be cautious as the mixture will bubble vigorously.
4. **Pour Over Pretzels:**
    - Immediately pour the hot caramel mixture evenly over the pretzels on the baking sheet. Use a spatula to spread it out if needed.
5. **Melt Chocolate:**
    - In a microwave-safe bowl or using a double boiler, melt the chocolate chips until smooth and creamy, stirring frequently to prevent burning.
6. **Spread Chocolate:**
    - Pour the melted chocolate over the caramel layer, spreading it evenly with a spatula to cover.
7. **Sprinkle with Sea Salt:**
    - While the chocolate is still warm, sprinkle sea salt flakes evenly over the top for a sweet-salty contrast.
8. **Chill Until Set:**
    - Place the baking sheet in the refrigerator for about 1 hour, or until the bark is completely set and firm.
9. **Break Into Pieces:**
    - Once set, break the bark into pieces using your hands or a sharp knife.

10. **Store:**
    - Store the salted caramel pretzel bark in an airtight container at room temperature for up to 1 week, or in the refrigerator for longer shelf life.

Tips:

- Customize your bark by using different types of pretzels (mini twists, rods, or sticks) or adding chopped nuts like almonds or pecans.
- Adjust the amount of sea salt flakes based on your preference for saltiness.
- For a quicker setting time, place the bark in the freezer for about 30 minutes.

Enjoy this salted caramel pretzel bark as a delicious homemade treat or as a delightful gift for friends and family. It's perfect for satisfying sweet and salty cravings!

Apple Turnovers

Ingredients:

For the Pastry:

- 2 sheets puff pastry, thawed if frozen
- Flour, for dusting

For the Apple Filling:

- 2 large apples (such as Granny Smith or Honeycrisp), peeled, cored, and diced
- 2 tablespoons unsalted butter
- 1/4 cup packed brown sugar
- 1 teaspoon ground cinnamon
- 1/4 teaspoon ground nutmeg (optional)
- 1 tablespoon lemon juice
- 1 tablespoon cornstarch
- Pinch of salt

For Assembly:

- 1 egg, beaten (for egg wash)
- Granulated sugar, for sprinkling

Instructions:

1. **Prepare the Apple Filling:**
   - In a medium saucepan, melt the butter over medium heat. Add the diced apples, brown sugar, cinnamon, nutmeg (if using), lemon juice, cornstarch, and a pinch of salt.
   - Cook the mixture, stirring occasionally, until the apples are tender and the sauce has thickened, about 5-7 minutes. Remove from heat and let cool slightly.
2. **Preheat the Oven:**
   - Preheat your oven to 375°F (190°C). Line a baking sheet with parchment paper or a silicone baking mat.
3. **Roll Out the Pastry:**
   - Lightly flour your work surface and roll out each sheet of puff pastry to a 12x12-inch square. Cut each square into 4 equal squares.
4. **Fill the Turnovers:**

    - Spoon a generous tablespoon of the apple filling onto one half of each pastry square, leaving a border around the edges.
5. **Fold and Seal:**
    - Fold the other half of each pastry square over the filling to create a triangle. Press the edges firmly with a fork to seal. Trim any excess dough if necessary.
6. **Egg Wash and Bake:**
    - Place the turnovers on the prepared baking sheet. Brush the tops with beaten egg and sprinkle with granulated sugar.
7. **Bake:**
    - Bake in the preheated oven for 20-25 minutes, or until the turnovers are golden brown and puffed up.
8. **Cool and Serve:**
    - Remove from the oven and let the turnovers cool slightly on the baking sheet before transferring them to a wire rack to cool completely.
9. **Optional: Glaze (if desired):**
    - For a sweeter touch, you can drizzle the cooled turnovers with a simple glaze made from powdered sugar and a little milk or water.

Tips:

- Ensure the apple filling is cooled slightly before spooning onto the pastry to prevent it from melting the dough.
- Feel free to add raisins, chopped nuts, or a dash of vanilla extract to the apple filling for extra flavor.
- Serve warm or at room temperature, and store any leftovers in an airtight container at room temperature for up to 2 days.

These apple turnovers are perfect for breakfast, brunch, or dessert. They're flaky, fruity, and irresistibly delicious—a true treat for apple lovers!

Gingerbread Cookies

Ingredients:

For the Cookie Dough:

- 3 cups all-purpose flour
- 1 teaspoon baking soda
- 1/4 teaspoon salt
- 1 tablespoon ground ginger
- 1 1/2 teaspoons ground cinnamon
- 1/2 teaspoon ground cloves
- 1/2 teaspoon ground nutmeg
- 3/4 cup unsalted butter, softened
- 1/2 cup granulated sugar
- 1/2 cup packed brown sugar
- 1 large egg
- 1/2 cup molasses
- 1 teaspoon vanilla extract

For Decorating:

- Royal icing, sprinkles, or candies (optional)

Instructions:

1. **Preheat the Oven:**
   - Preheat your oven to 350°F (175°C). Line baking sheets with parchment paper or silicone baking mats.
2. **Mix Dry Ingredients:**
   - In a medium bowl, whisk together the flour, baking soda, salt, ginger, cinnamon, cloves, and nutmeg. Set aside.
3. **Cream Butter and Sugars:**
   - In a large bowl or using a stand mixer fitted with the paddle attachment, beat the softened butter, granulated sugar, and brown sugar until light and fluffy.
4. **Add Egg and Molasses:**
   - Add the egg, molasses, and vanilla extract to the butter-sugar mixture. Beat until well combined.
5. **Combine Wet and Dry Ingredients:**

- Gradually add the dry ingredients to the wet ingredients, mixing until the dough comes together. If the dough seems too sticky, you can add a little more flour, a tablespoon at a time, until it reaches a firmer consistency.
6. **Chill the Dough (Optional):**
    - Wrap the dough in plastic wrap and refrigerate for at least 1 hour or overnight. Chilling the dough helps the flavors develop and makes it easier to roll out.
7. **Roll Out the Dough:**
    - On a lightly floured surface, roll out the dough to about 1/4-inch thickness. Use gingerbread cookie cutters to cut out shapes. Place the cut-out cookies onto the prepared baking sheets, spacing them about 1 inch apart.
8. **Bake the Cookies:**
    - Bake in the preheated oven for 8-10 minutes, or until the edges are firm and lightly browned. Be careful not to overbake, as gingerbread cookies should be slightly soft when removed from the oven.
9. **Cool and Decorate:**
    - Let the cookies cool on the baking sheets for a few minutes before transferring them to a wire rack to cool completely.
    - Once cooled, decorate the gingerbread cookies with royal icing, sprinkles, or candies as desired. Allow the icing to set before storing or serving.

Tips:

- For a softer cookie, bake them for slightly less time.
- If you prefer a spicier cookie, you can increase the amount of ground ginger or add a pinch of black pepper.
- Store decorated gingerbread cookies in an airtight container at room temperature for up to 1 week.

Enjoy these homemade gingerbread cookies as a festive treat during the holiday season or anytime you crave a taste of warm spices and sweetness!

Apricot Bars

Ingredients:

For the Crust:

- 1 cup all-purpose flour
- 1/2 cup unsalted butter, softened
- 1/4 cup granulated sugar
- 1/4 teaspoon salt

For the Apricot Filling:

- 1 1/2 cups dried apricots
- 1/2 cup water
- 1/4 cup granulated sugar
- 1 tablespoon lemon juice
- 1/2 teaspoon vanilla extract

Instructions:

1. **Preheat the Oven:**
    - Preheat your oven to 350°F (175°C). Grease or line an 8x8-inch baking pan with parchment paper, leaving an overhang on the sides for easy removal.
2. **Make the Apricot Filling:**
    - In a small saucepan, combine the dried apricots and water. Bring to a boil over medium-high heat, then reduce the heat to low and simmer for about 10 minutes, or until the apricots are softened and the liquid is mostly absorbed.
    - Stir in the granulated sugar, lemon juice, and vanilla extract. Cook for another 2-3 minutes, stirring constantly, until the mixture thickens slightly. Remove from heat and let it cool slightly.
3. **Prepare the Crust:**
    - In a mixing bowl, combine the softened butter, flour, sugar, and salt. Use a pastry cutter or your hands to mix until crumbly and the butter is fully incorporated.
4. **Assemble the Bars:**
    - Press about two-thirds of the crust mixture evenly into the bottom of the prepared baking pan. Press down firmly to create an even layer.
5. **Spread the Apricot Filling:**
    - Spread the apricot filling evenly over the crust layer in the baking pan.

6. **Top with Remaining Crust:**
   - Sprinkle the remaining crust mixture evenly over the apricot filling. Press lightly with your fingers.
7. **Bake:**
   - Bake in the preheated oven for 25-30 minutes, or until the crust is golden brown.
8. **Cool and Slice:**
   - Allow the apricot bars to cool completely in the pan on a wire rack. Once cooled, use the parchment paper overhang to lift the bars out of the pan. Transfer to a cutting board and slice into bars or squares.
9. **Serve:**
   - Serve the apricot bars as they are or dust with powdered sugar for a decorative touch.

Tips:

- You can substitute other dried fruits such as dates, figs, or cranberries for a variation on these bars.
- Store leftover apricot bars in an airtight container at room temperature for up to 5 days, or refrigerate for longer freshness.

These apricot bars are wonderfully sweet, tangy, and make a perfect snack or dessert for any occasion. Enjoy their fruity goodness with friends and family!

Tiramisu

Ingredients:

- 1 cup strong brewed coffee, cooled
- 2 tablespoons coffee liqueur (optional)
- 24-30 ladyfinger biscuits (savoiardi)
- 4 large egg yolks
- 1/2 cup granulated sugar
- 1 cup mascarpone cheese, softened
- 1 cup heavy cream
- 1 teaspoon vanilla extract
- Unsweetened cocoa powder, for dusting

Instructions:

1. **Prepare Coffee Mixture:**
   - In a shallow dish, combine the cooled brewed coffee and coffee liqueur (if using). Mix well and set aside.
2. **Make Mascarpone Mixture:**
   - In a large mixing bowl, beat the egg yolks and sugar until pale and creamy. Add the mascarpone cheese and mix until smooth and well combined.
3. **Whip Heavy Cream:**
   - In another bowl, whip the heavy cream and vanilla extract until stiff peaks form.
4. **Combine Mascarpone and Cream:**
   - Gently fold the whipped cream into the mascarpone mixture until smooth and creamy. Be careful not to overmix.
5. **Assemble the Tiramisu:**
   - Quickly dip each ladyfinger biscuit into the coffee mixture, ensuring they are soaked but not overly soggy. Arrange a layer of soaked biscuits in the bottom of a 9x9-inch square dish or a similar-sized serving dish.
6. **Layering:**
   - Spread half of the mascarpone mixture evenly over the layer of biscuits.
7. **Repeat Layers:**
   - Create another layer with the remaining soaked biscuits, followed by the remaining mascarpone mixture on top.
8. **Chill:**
   - Cover the tiramisu with plastic wrap and refrigerate for at least 4 hours, or ideally overnight, to allow the flavors to meld and the dessert to set.

9. **Serve:**
    - Before serving, dust the top of the tiramisu generously with unsweetened cocoa powder using a fine mesh sieve.

Tips:

- Ensure the coffee mixture is cooled to room temperature before dipping the ladyfingers to prevent them from becoming too soggy.
- For a non-alcoholic version, you can omit the coffee liqueur or substitute with a small amount of vanilla extract mixed into the coffee.
- Tiramisu can be stored covered in the refrigerator for up to 3 days. The flavors often improve as it chills, making it a perfect make-ahead dessert for gatherings.

Enjoy this classic tiramisu with its creamy, coffee-infused layers and delicate dusting of cocoa—a perfect ending to any meal or special occasion!

Mint Chocolate Chip Ice Cream

Ingredients:

- 2 cups heavy cream
- 1 cup whole milk
- 3/4 cup granulated sugar
- 1/4 teaspoon salt
- 1 teaspoon pure vanilla extract
- 1 teaspoon peppermint extract
- Green food coloring (optional)
- 3/4 cup chocolate chips or chopped chocolate (semisweet or dark)

Instructions:

1. **Prepare the Ice Cream Base:**
    - In a mixing bowl, whisk together the heavy cream, whole milk, sugar, salt, vanilla extract, and peppermint extract until the sugar is dissolved.
2. **Add Green Food Coloring (Optional):**
    - If desired, add a few drops of green food coloring to achieve a minty green color. Mix well.
3. **Chill the Mixture:**
    - Cover the bowl with plastic wrap and refrigerate the mixture for at least 2 hours, or overnight, to chill thoroughly.
4. **Freeze in Ice Cream Maker:**
    - Once chilled, pour the mixture into your ice cream maker and churn according to the manufacturer's instructions until it reaches a soft-serve consistency.
5. **Add Chocolate Chips:**
    - During the last few minutes of churning, add the chocolate chips or chopped chocolate. Let the ice cream maker incorporate them evenly.
6. **Transfer and Freeze:**
    - Transfer the churned ice cream into a freezer-safe container. Smooth the top with a spatula and cover tightly with a lid or plastic wrap.
7. **Finish Freezing:**
    - Freeze the mint chocolate chip ice cream for at least 4 hours, or until firm, before serving.
8. **Serve:**
    - Scoop the mint chocolate chip ice cream into bowls or cones. Enjoy it as is or garnish with additional chocolate chips or mint leaves for decoration.

Tips:

- For a stronger mint flavor, adjust the amount of peppermint extract to your taste.
- Ensure your ice cream maker bowl is properly frozen before churning to achieve the best texture.
- If you prefer smaller chocolate pieces, use mini chocolate chips or finely chopped chocolate.

Homemade mint chocolate chip ice cream is a delightful treat for summer or any time you crave a cool and creamy dessert with a burst of refreshing mint and chocolate in every bite!

Nutella Crepes

Ingredients:

For the Crepe Batter:

- 1 cup all-purpose flour
- 2 large eggs
- 1 cup milk
- 1/4 cup water
- 2 tablespoons unsalted butter, melted
- 2 tablespoons granulated sugar (optional)
- 1/2 teaspoon vanilla extract
- Pinch of salt

For Filling and Serving:

- Nutella (or any hazelnut chocolate spread)
- Fresh berries (strawberries, raspberries) for garnish (optional)
- Powdered sugar for dusting (optional)

Instructions:

1. **Make the Crepe Batter:**
   - In a mixing bowl, whisk together the flour, eggs, milk, water, melted butter, sugar (if using), vanilla extract, and salt until smooth and well combined. The batter should be thin, similar to the consistency of heavy cream. Let the batter rest for 15-30 minutes.
2. **Cook the Crepes:**
   - Heat a non-stick crepe pan or skillet over medium heat. Lightly grease the pan with butter or cooking spray.
   - Pour about 1/4 cup of batter into the center of the pan, swirling it around quickly to spread the batter evenly in a thin layer across the bottom of the pan.
   - Cook the crepe for about 1-2 minutes, or until the edges begin to lift and the bottom is lightly golden. Use a spatula to flip the crepe and cook for another 30 seconds to 1 minute on the other side. Remove the cooked crepe from the pan and repeat with the remaining batter, stacking the cooked crepes on a plate.
3. **Assemble the Crepes:**

- Spread a generous amount of Nutella (or hazelnut chocolate spread of your choice) evenly over one half of each crepe. Fold the crepe in half, then fold it in half again to form a triangle or roll it up.
4. **Serve:**
    - Arrange the Nutella crepes on serving plates. Dust with powdered sugar if desired and garnish with fresh berries.

Tips:

- Crepes can be made ahead of time and stored stacked with parchment paper between each crepe. Reheat gently in a skillet or microwave before filling.
- Experiment with other fillings such as sliced bananas, whipped cream, or even a drizzle of caramel sauce in addition to Nutella.

Enjoy these Nutella crepes for breakfast, brunch, or as a decadent dessert. They are versatile and sure to be a hit with chocolate lovers of all ages!

Chocolate Covered Strawberries

Ingredients:

- Fresh strawberries, washed and dried (about 1 pound)
- 8 ounces (225g) semi-sweet or dark chocolate, chopped
- 1 tablespoon coconut oil or vegetable shortening (optional, for thinning the chocolate)
- Optional toppings: chopped nuts, sprinkles, shredded coconut, etc.

Instructions:

1. **Prepare the Strawberries:**
   - Wash the strawberries under cold water and gently pat them dry with paper towels or a clean kitchen towel. Make sure they are completely dry before dipping in chocolate, as water can cause the chocolate to seize.
2. **Melt the Chocolate:**
   - Place the chopped chocolate in a microwave-safe bowl. Microwave in 30-second intervals, stirring each time, until the chocolate is melted and smooth. Be careful not to overheat the chocolate.
3. **Add Coconut Oil (Optional):**
   - If the chocolate seems too thick for dipping, stir in coconut oil or vegetable shortening to thin it out slightly. This will help create a smoother coating on the strawberries.
4. **Dip the Strawberries:**
   - Hold a strawberry by the stem and dip it into the melted chocolate, swirling to coat it completely. Allow any excess chocolate to drip back into the bowl.
5. **Set on Parchment Paper:**
   - Place the dipped strawberry onto a parchment-lined baking sheet or tray. Repeat with the remaining strawberries.
6. **Add Toppings (Optional):**
   - If desired, sprinkle the chocolate-covered strawberries with chopped nuts, sprinkles, shredded coconut, or any other toppings while the chocolate is still wet.
7. **Chill:**
   - Place the tray of chocolate-covered strawberries in the refrigerator for about 15-30 minutes, or until the chocolate is set and firm.
8. **Serve:**

- - Arrange the chocolate-covered strawberries on a serving platter and enjoy immediately as a decadent dessert or treat.

Tips:

- Use high-quality chocolate for the best flavor and texture. Dark or semi-sweet chocolate works well, but you can also use milk chocolate if you prefer.
- Experiment with different toppings to customize your chocolate-covered strawberries to your liking.
- Store leftover chocolate-covered strawberries in an airtight container in the refrigerator. Enjoy them within 1-2 days for the best quality.

These homemade chocolate-covered strawberries are not only delicious but also make a stunning presentation for parties, romantic occasions, or as a special homemade gift. Enjoy the combination of juicy strawberries and rich, smooth chocolate!

Kiwi Lime Pie

Ingredients:

For the Crust:

- 1 1/2 cups graham cracker crumbs (about 10-12 graham crackers)
- 6 tablespoons unsalted butter, melted
- 1/4 cup granulated sugar

For the Filling:

- 1 can (14 ounces) sweetened condensed milk
- 4 large egg yolks
- 1/2 cup fresh lime juice (about 4-5 limes)
- Zest of 1 lime
- 3 ripe kiwi fruits, peeled and chopped

For Garnish (Optional):

- Whipped cream
- Sliced kiwi fruits
- Lime zest

Instructions:

1. **Preheat the Oven:**
   - Preheat your oven to 350°F (175°C).
2. **Make the Crust:**
   - In a mixing bowl, combine the graham cracker crumbs, melted butter, and granulated sugar. Mix until the crumbs are evenly coated with butter.
3. **Press into Pie Pan:**
   - Press the crumb mixture firmly and evenly into the bottom and up the sides of a 9-inch pie pan or dish. Use the bottom of a measuring cup or glass to compact the crumbs.
4. **Bake the Crust:**
   - Bake the crust in the preheated oven for 8-10 minutes, or until lightly golden and set. Remove from the oven and let it cool slightly while you prepare the filling.
5. **Prepare the Filling:**

- In a large mixing bowl, whisk together the sweetened condensed milk and egg yolks until smooth.
- Gradually whisk in the lime juice and lime zest until well combined.

6. **Add Kiwi Fruit:**
   - Gently fold in the chopped kiwi fruits into the lime mixture.
7. **Assemble and Bake:**
   - Pour the filling mixture into the baked graham cracker crust, spreading it evenly.
8. **Bake the Pie:**
   - Bake the pie in the preheated oven for 15-18 minutes, or until the center is set but still slightly jiggly.
9. **Chill:**
   - Remove the pie from the oven and let it cool completely on a wire rack. Once cooled, refrigerate the pie for at least 2-3 hours, or until well-chilled and set.
10. **Serve:**
    - Before serving, garnish the Kiwi Lime Pie with whipped cream, sliced kiwi fruits, and additional lime zest if desired.

Tips:

- Use ripe kiwi fruits for the best flavor and texture in the pie filling.
- If you prefer a smoother texture, you can puree the kiwi fruits instead of chopping them.
- Store leftover Kiwi Lime Pie covered in the refrigerator for up to 3 days.

Enjoy this tropical and tangy Kiwi Lime Pie as a refreshing dessert that's perfect for summer gatherings or any occasion where you want to impress with a unique and delicious treat!

Pomegranate Panna Cotta

Ingredients:

For the Panna Cotta:

- 2 cups heavy cream
- 1/2 cup granulated sugar
- 1 teaspoon vanilla extract
- 1 envelope (about 2 1/4 teaspoons) powdered gelatin
- 1/4 cup cold water

For the Pomegranate Sauce:

- 1 cup pomegranate juice (freshly squeezed or bottled)
- 1/4 cup granulated sugar
- 1 tablespoon cornstarch
- 1 tablespoon cold water
- Fresh pomegranate arils for garnish (optional)

Instructions:

1. **Prepare the Panna Cotta:**
    - In a saucepan, combine the heavy cream and granulated sugar over medium heat. Stir until the sugar is dissolved and the mixture is just beginning to simmer. Remove from heat and stir in the vanilla extract.
    - In a small bowl, sprinkle the gelatin over 1/4 cup of cold water. Let it sit for about 5 minutes to soften.
    - After the gelatin has softened, stir it into the warm cream mixture until completely dissolved.
2. **Pour into Molds:**
    - Divide the panna cotta mixture evenly among 4-6 serving glasses or ramekins. Allow them to cool to room temperature, then cover with plastic wrap and refrigerate for at least 4 hours, or until set.
3. **Make the Pomegranate Sauce:**
    - In a small saucepan, combine the pomegranate juice and granulated sugar over medium heat. Stir until the sugar is dissolved and the mixture begins to simmer.
    - In a small bowl, mix the cornstarch with 1 tablespoon of cold water to create a slurry. Slowly whisk the cornstarch slurry into the simmering pomegranate mixture.

        - Continue to cook, stirring constantly, until the sauce has thickened and coats the back of a spoon (about 3-4 minutes). Remove from heat and let it cool to room temperature.
4. **Assemble and Serve:**
        - Once the panna cotta has set, spoon a layer of the cooled pomegranate sauce over each serving. If desired, garnish with fresh pomegranate arils.
5. **Chill and Enjoy:**
        - Return the assembled panna cotta to the refrigerator for at least 30 minutes to allow the sauce to set slightly.
6. **Serve Cold:**
        - Serve the Pomegranate Panna Cotta chilled and enjoy the creamy texture with the refreshing burst of pomegranate flavor.

Tips:

- To unmold the panna cotta easily, dip the bottoms of the ramekins or glasses into warm water for a few seconds, then run a knife around the edge of each panna cotta to loosen it before inverting onto a serving plate.
- Adjust the sweetness of the pomegranate sauce to your taste by adding more or less sugar.
- Pomegranate arils not only add a pop of color but also provide a delightful crunch to the dessert.

This Pomegranate Panna Cotta is sure to impress with its creamy texture and vibrant flavors, making it a perfect dessert for special occasions or any time you crave something indulgent and sophisticated.

Mocha Cheesecake Bars

Ingredients:

For the Crust:

- 1 1/2 cups chocolate cookie crumbs (about 20-24 cookies)
- 6 tablespoons unsalted butter, melted
- 1/4 cup granulated sugar

For the Cheesecake Filling:

- 16 ounces (2 packages) cream cheese, softened
- 1/2 cup granulated sugar
- 2 large eggs
- 1 tablespoon all-purpose flour
- 1/2 cup sour cream
- 1 tablespoon instant coffee granules or espresso powder, dissolved in 1 tablespoon hot water
- 1 teaspoon vanilla extract

For the Mocha Swirl:

- 1/4 cup semi-sweet chocolate chips
- 1 tablespoon heavy cream
- 1 tablespoon instant coffee granules or espresso powder

Instructions:

1. **Preheat the Oven:**
   - Preheat your oven to 325°F (160°C). Line an 8x8-inch baking pan with parchment paper, leaving an overhang on the sides for easy removal.
2. **Make the Crust:**
   - In a medium bowl, combine the chocolate cookie crumbs, melted butter, and granulated sugar. Mix until the crumbs are evenly coated with butter.
   - Press the mixture firmly and evenly into the bottom of the prepared baking pan.
3. **Prepare the Cheesecake Filling:**
   - In a large mixing bowl, beat the softened cream cheese and granulated sugar until smooth and creamy.
   - Add the eggs one at a time, beating well after each addition.

- Mix in the flour, sour cream, dissolved coffee (coffee granules dissolved in hot water), and vanilla extract until smooth and well combined.
4. **Make the Mocha Swirl:**
    - In a small microwave-safe bowl, combine the chocolate chips and heavy cream. Microwave in 20-30 second intervals, stirring each time, until the chocolate is melted and smooth.
    - Stir in the instant coffee granules or espresso powder until dissolved and well combined.
5. **Assemble the Bars:**
    - Pour the cheesecake filling over the prepared crust in the baking pan, spreading it into an even layer.
    - Drop spoonfuls of the mocha swirl mixture over the top of the cheesecake filling.
6. **Swirl the Layers:**
    - Use a knife or toothpick to swirl the mocha mixture into the cheesecake filling to create a marbled effect.
7. **Bake:**
    - Bake the Mocha Cheesecake Bars in the preheated oven for 35-40 minutes, or until the edges are set and the center is slightly jiggly.
8. **Cool and Chill:**
    - Remove the pan from the oven and let the cheesecake bars cool completely on a wire rack. Once cooled, refrigerate for at least 3-4 hours, or until well-chilled and firm.
9. **Slice and Serve:**
    - Lift the chilled cheesecake bars out of the pan using the parchment paper overhang. Cut into squares and serve chilled.

Tips:

- For the chocolate cookie crumbs, you can use store-bought chocolate graham crackers or chocolate sandwich cookies (filling removed).
- Ensure the cream cheese is softened to room temperature for a smooth and creamy cheesecake filling.
- Store leftover Mocha Cheesecake Bars covered in the refrigerator for up to 3-4 days.

These Mocha Cheesecake Bars are perfect for coffee and chocolate lovers alike, combining creamy cheesecake with the rich flavors of mocha for a decadent and satisfying dessert experience. Enjoy these bars as a delightful treat for special occasions or any time you crave something indulgent!

Banana Cream Pie

Ingredients:

For the Crust:

- 1 1/2 cups graham cracker crumbs (about 10-12 graham crackers)
- 6 tablespoons unsalted butter, melted
- 1/4 cup granulated sugar

For the Filling:

- 2/3 cup granulated sugar
- 1/4 cup cornstarch
- 1/2 teaspoon salt
- 3 cups whole milk
- 4 large egg yolks
- 2 tablespoons unsalted butter
- 1 1/2 teaspoons vanilla extract
- 3 ripe bananas, sliced

For the Whipped Cream Topping:

- 1 cup heavy cream
- 2 tablespoons powdered sugar
- 1/2 teaspoon vanilla extract

Instructions:

1. **Make the Crust:**
   - Preheat your oven to 350°F (175°C). In a mixing bowl, combine the graham cracker crumbs, melted butter, and granulated sugar until well combined.
   - Press the mixture firmly and evenly into the bottom and up the sides of a 9-inch pie dish or pan. Use the back of a spoon or measuring cup to compact the crumbs.
   - Bake the crust in the preheated oven for 10-12 minutes, or until lightly golden and set. Remove from the oven and let it cool completely on a wire rack.
2. **Prepare the Filling:**
   - In a medium saucepan, whisk together the granulated sugar, cornstarch, and salt. Gradually whisk in the milk until smooth.

- Cook over medium heat, stirring constantly, until the mixture thickens and comes to a boil (about 8-10 minutes).
- In a separate bowl, whisk the egg yolks. Gradually whisk in about 1/2 cup of the hot milk mixture to temper the eggs.
- Gradually add the tempered egg mixture back into the saucepan with the remaining milk mixture, whisking constantly. Cook for another 2-3 minutes, stirring constantly, until thickened.
- Remove from heat and stir in the butter and vanilla extract until smooth and well combined.

3. **Assemble the Pie:**
    - Arrange half of the sliced bananas over the bottom of the cooled graham cracker crust.
    - Pour half of the warm custard filling over the bananas, spreading it into an even layer.
    - Arrange the remaining sliced bananas over the custard filling.
    - Pour the remaining custard filling over the bananas, spreading it into an even layer. Smooth the top with a spatula.
4. **Chill the Pie:**
    - Cover the pie with plastic wrap, pressing it directly onto the surface of the custard to prevent a skin from forming.
    - Refrigerate the Banana Cream Pie for at least 4 hours, or until well-chilled and set.
5. **Make the Whipped Cream Topping:**
    - In a mixing bowl, whip the heavy cream, powdered sugar, and vanilla extract until stiff peaks form.
6. **Serve:**
    - Remove the chilled pie from the refrigerator. Spread or pipe the whipped cream over the top of the pie.
    - Optionally, garnish with additional banana slices or grated chocolate.
7. **Slice and Enjoy:**
    - Slice the Banana Cream Pie and serve chilled. Enjoy the creamy custard, fresh bananas, and buttery graham cracker crust!

Tips:

- Ensure the custard filling is thickened properly before pouring over the bananas to prevent a runny pie.
- For a decorative touch, reserve a few banana slices and arrange them on top of the whipped cream before serving.

- Store leftover Banana Cream Pie covered in the refrigerator for up to 2-3 days.

This Banana Cream Pie is a classic dessert that's perfect for any occasion, combining creamy texture with delightful banana flavor and a buttery crust. Enjoy it as a refreshing treat that's sure to impress!

Raspberry Chocolate Tart

Ingredients:

For the Chocolate Tart Shell:

- 1 1/2 cups all-purpose flour
- 1/2 cup unsweetened cocoa powder
- 1/2 cup powdered sugar
- 1/4 teaspoon salt
- 3/4 cup unsalted butter, cold and cut into cubes
- 1 large egg yolk
- 2-4 tablespoons ice water

For the Chocolate Ganache Filling:

- 1 cup heavy cream
- 8 ounces semi-sweet chocolate, chopped (or chocolate chips)
- 1 teaspoon vanilla extract

For the Raspberry Topping:

- 2 cups fresh raspberries
- 1/4 cup seedless raspberry jam, melted
- Fresh mint leaves, for garnish (optional)

Instructions:

1. **Make the Chocolate Tart Shell:**
   - In a food processor, combine the flour, cocoa powder, powdered sugar, and salt. Pulse a few times to mix.
   - Add the cold cubed butter and pulse until the mixture resembles coarse crumbs.
   - Add the egg yolk and pulse again until the dough starts to come together.
   - Gradually add the ice water, 1 tablespoon at a time, pulsing after each addition, until the dough holds together when pinched with your fingers.
   - Turn the dough out onto a lightly floured surface and gently knead a few times to bring it together into a ball. Flatten into a disc, wrap in plastic wrap, and refrigerate for at least 30 minutes.
   - Preheat your oven to 375°F (190°C).

- On a lightly floured surface, roll out the chilled dough into a circle about 12 inches in diameter and 1/4 inch thick.
- Carefully transfer the rolled-out dough to a 9-inch tart pan with a removable bottom. Press the dough into the bottom and up the sides of the pan. Trim any excess dough from the edges.
- Prick the bottom of the tart shell with a fork. Line the shell with parchment paper or aluminum foil and fill with pie weights or dried beans.
- Bake the tart shell in the preheated oven for 15 minutes. Remove the parchment paper and weights and bake for an additional 5-7 minutes, or until the crust is set and dry to the touch.
- Remove from the oven and let the tart shell cool completely on a wire rack.

2. **Prepare the Chocolate Ganache Filling:**
    - In a small saucepan, heat the heavy cream over medium heat until it just begins to simmer (do not boil).
    - Remove from heat and add the chopped chocolate (or chocolate chips) to the hot cream. Let it sit for 1-2 minutes to soften.
    - Stir the mixture gently until the chocolate is completely melted and smooth. Stir in the vanilla extract until well combined.
    - Pour the chocolate ganache into the cooled tart shell. Spread it evenly with a spatula. Let it cool slightly.

3. **Assemble the Tart:**
    - Arrange the fresh raspberries over the top of the chocolate ganache filling in a single layer, covering the entire surface.
    - Brush the melted raspberry jam over the raspberries to glaze.

4. **Chill and Serve:**
    - Refrigerate the Raspberry Chocolate Tart for at least 1 hour, or until the ganache is set.
    - Before serving, garnish with fresh mint leaves if desired.

5. **Slice and Enjoy:**
    - Slice the tart with a sharp knife and serve chilled. Enjoy the decadent combination of chocolate, raspberries, and buttery tart shell!

Tips:

- Use high-quality chocolate for the best flavor in the ganache.
- Ensure the tart shell is fully cooled before adding the ganache to prevent it from melting.
- Store any leftover Raspberry Chocolate Tart covered in the refrigerator for up to 3 days.

This Raspberry Chocolate Tart is a perfect dessert for special occasions or any time you want to impress with a stunning and delicious treat. Enjoy the rich chocolate ganache paired with the bright and tangy raspberries for a delightful flavor experience!

Lemon Thyme Shortbread

Ingredients:

- 1 cup unsalted butter, softened
- 1/2 cup powdered sugar
- 2 cups all-purpose flour
- Zest of 1 lemon
- 1 tablespoon fresh thyme leaves, finely chopped
- 1/4 teaspoon salt
- Additional powdered sugar for dusting (optional)

Instructions:

1. **Preheat and Prepare:**
    - Preheat your oven to 325°F (160°C). Line a baking sheet with parchment paper.
2. **Cream Butter and Sugar:**
    - In a large mixing bowl, cream together the softened butter and powdered sugar until light and fluffy.
3. **Add Flavorings:**
    - Stir in the lemon zest, chopped thyme leaves, and salt until well combined.
4. **Incorporate Flour:**
    - Gradually add the flour to the butter mixture, mixing until a dough forms. The dough should come together and be slightly crumbly but hold its shape when pressed.
5. **Shape the Dough:**
    - Turn the dough out onto a lightly floured surface and gently knead a few times to bring it together.
    - Shape the dough into a smooth ball or log. If making slice-and-bake cookies, shape the dough into a log about 2 inches in diameter. If using cookie cutters, flatten the dough into a disc about 1/2 inch thick.
6. **Cut or Shape:**
    - For slice-and-bake cookies, slice the log into rounds about 1/4 inch thick. For shaped cookies, use cookie cutters to cut out desired shapes.
7. **Bake:**
    - Place the shortbread cookies on the prepared baking sheet, spacing them about 1 inch apart.
    - Bake in the preheated oven for 12-15 minutes, or until the edges are lightly golden. The shortbread should be firm to the touch but not browned.

8. **Cool:**
    - Remove the shortbread from the oven and let them cool on the baking sheet for 5 minutes.
    - Transfer the cookies to a wire rack to cool completely.
9. **Optional Dusting:**
    - Once cooled, dust the tops of the shortbread cookies with powdered sugar for an added touch of sweetness (optional).
10. **Serve and Enjoy:**
    - Serve the Lemon Thyme Shortbread cookies with tea or coffee, or enjoy them as a delightful treat any time of day.

Tips:

- Ensure the butter is softened but not melted for the best texture.
- If you prefer a stronger lemon flavor, you can add a few drops of lemon extract or a bit more lemon zest.
- Store the cooled shortbread cookies in an airtight container at room temperature for up to one week.

These Lemon Thyme Shortbread cookies are perfect for serving as a snack or dessert, offering a delicate balance of citrusy zest and herbal fragrance in each buttery bite. Enjoy making and sharing these delightful cookies with family and friends!

Pineapple Coconut Cupcakes

Ingredients:

For the Cupcakes:

- 1 1/2 cups all-purpose flour
- 1 teaspoon baking powder
- 1/4 teaspoon baking soda
- 1/4 teaspoon salt
- 1/2 cup unsalted butter, softened
- 1 cup granulated sugar
- 2 large eggs, room temperature
- 1/2 cup canned crushed pineapple, drained (reserve juice for frosting)
- 1/2 cup shredded coconut
- 1/2 cup buttermilk
- 1 teaspoon vanilla extract

For the Coconut Frosting:

- 1/2 cup unsalted butter, softened
- 3 cups powdered sugar
- 1/4 cup canned pineapple juice (reserved from crushed pineapple)
- 1/2 teaspoon coconut extract
- 1/2 cup shredded coconut, toasted (for garnish)

Instructions:

1. **Preheat and Prepare:**
    - Preheat your oven to 350°F (175°C). Line a muffin tin with paper cupcake liners.
2. **Mix Dry Ingredients:**
    - In a medium bowl, whisk together the flour, baking powder, baking soda, and salt. Set aside.
3. **Cream Butter and Sugar:**
    - In a large mixing bowl, cream together the softened butter and granulated sugar until light and fluffy.
4. **Add Eggs and Flavorings:**
    - Beat in the eggs one at a time, scraping down the sides of the bowl as needed.
5. **Combine Wet and Dry Ingredients:**

- Add the crushed pineapple and shredded coconut to the butter mixture, mixing until combined.
- Gradually add the dry ingredients to the butter mixture alternately with the buttermilk, beginning and ending with the dry ingredients. Mix until just combined.

6. **Bake:**
   - Divide the batter evenly among the prepared cupcake liners, filling each about 2/3 full.
   - Bake in the preheated oven for 18-20 minutes, or until a toothpick inserted into the center comes out clean.

7. **Cool:**
   - Remove the cupcakes from the muffin tin and transfer them to a wire rack to cool completely before frosting.

8. **Make the Coconut Frosting:**
   - In a large mixing bowl, beat the softened butter until creamy.
   - Gradually add the powdered sugar, one cup at a time, beating well after each addition.
   - Add the pineapple juice and coconut extract, mixing until smooth and fluffy.

9. **Frost the Cupcakes:**
   - Once the cupcakes are completely cool, frost them with the coconut frosting using a piping bag or offset spatula.

10. **Garnish:**
    - Sprinkle toasted shredded coconut over the frosted cupcakes for decoration.

11. **Serve and Enjoy:**
    - Serve the Pineapple Coconut Cupcakes immediately, or store them in an airtight container in the refrigerator for up to 3 days.

Tips:

- To toast shredded coconut, spread it evenly on a baking sheet and bake at 325°F (160°C) for 5-7 minutes, stirring occasionally, until lightly golden brown.
- Ensure the crushed pineapple is well-drained to prevent excess moisture in the cupcake batter.
- For an extra burst of flavor, you can add a small amount of pineapple extract to the cupcake batter or frosting.

These Pineapple Coconut Cupcakes are a delightful treat with tropical flavors that are perfect for parties, gatherings, or simply indulging in a sweet moment. Enjoy the combination of pineapple and coconut in every bite!

Pistachio Baklava

Ingredients:

For the Baklava:

- 1 package (16 oz) phyllo dough, thawed if frozen
- 1 1/2 cups unsalted pistachios, finely chopped
- 1 cup unsalted butter, melted

For the Syrup:

- 1 cup water
- 1 cup granulated sugar
- 1/2 cup honey
- 1 tablespoon lemon juice
- 1 cinnamon stick (optional)

Instructions:

1. **Prepare the Syrup:**
    - In a saucepan, combine water, granulated sugar, honey, lemon juice, and a cinnamon stick (if using). Bring to a boil over medium-high heat, stirring occasionally.
    - Reduce heat to low and simmer for 10-15 minutes, until the syrup slightly thickens. Remove from heat and let it cool. Once cooled, discard the cinnamon stick.
2. **Prepare the Pistachio Filling:**
    - In a bowl, mix together the finely chopped pistachios. Set aside.
3. **Assemble the Baklava:**
    - Preheat your oven to 350°F (175°C). Brush a 9x13-inch baking dish with melted butter.
    - Carefully unroll the phyllo dough and place it on a clean work surface. Cover with a slightly damp kitchen towel to prevent it from drying out.
    - Place one sheet of phyllo dough into the prepared baking dish and brush it generously with melted butter. Repeat with 7 more sheets of phyllo dough, brushing each layer with butter.
    - Sprinkle a generous amount of the pistachio filling evenly over the phyllo dough.

- Continue layering 8 more sheets of phyllo dough, brushing each layer with melted butter and sprinkling with pistachio filling. Finish with a top layer of 8 sheets of phyllo dough, brushing each layer with butter.

4. **Cut and Bake:**
    - Using a sharp knife, carefully cut the baklava into diamond or square shapes, cutting all the way through the layers.
    - Bake in the preheated oven for 45-50 minutes, or until the baklava is golden brown and crisp.
5. **Pour the Syrup:**
    - Remove the baklava from the oven and immediately pour the cooled syrup over the hot baklava, ensuring it covers all the cut lines.
6. **Cool and Serve:**
    - Allow the baklava to cool completely in the pan on a wire rack, allowing the phyllo to absorb the syrup.
    - Once cooled, carefully remove the pieces of baklava from the pan and serve on a platter.

Tips:

- Phyllo dough can dry out quickly, so keep it covered with a damp towel while assembling the baklava.
- For easier cutting, you can chill the baklava in the refrigerator for 1-2 hours after pouring the syrup.
- Store leftover baklava in an airtight container at room temperature for up to 1 week.

Enjoy this Pistachio Baklava with its layers of flaky pastry, crunchy pistachios, and sweet honey syrup—a delicious dessert that's perfect for special occasions or as a delightful treat with tea or coffee!

Mango Sticky Rice

Ingredients:

For the Sticky Rice:

- 1 cup Thai sticky rice (also known as glutinous rice or sweet rice)
- 1 cup coconut milk
- 1/2 cup water
- 1/4 teaspoon salt
- 2 tablespoons granulated sugar

For the Mango Topping:

- 2 ripe mangoes, peeled and sliced
- 1/2 cup coconut milk (for drizzling)
- 1 tablespoon sesame seeds, toasted (optional, for garnish)

Instructions:

1. **Prepare the Sticky Rice:**
   - Rinse the sticky rice under cold water until the water runs clear. This helps remove excess starch.
   - In a medium saucepan, combine the rinsed sticky rice with 1 cup of coconut milk, 1/2 cup of water, salt, and sugar. Stir to combine.
   - Bring the mixture to a boil over medium-high heat, stirring occasionally.
   - Once boiling, reduce the heat to low, cover with a lid, and simmer for 15-20 minutes, or until the rice is tender and all the liquid has been absorbed. Remove from heat and let it sit covered for 10 minutes to steam.
2. **Prepare the Mango:**
   - While the rice is cooking, peel and slice the mangoes into thin strips or cubes.
3. **Assemble the Mango Sticky Rice:**
   - Fluff the cooked sticky rice with a fork to separate the grains.
   - Place a portion of the sticky rice on a serving plate or bowl.
   - Arrange the sliced mangoes on top or alongside the sticky rice.
4. **Serve:**
   - Drizzle additional coconut milk over the mango and sticky rice.
   - Optionally, sprinkle toasted sesame seeds on top for added flavor and texture.
5. **Enjoy:**

- Serve the Mango Sticky Rice warm or at room temperature.

Tips:

- Thai sticky rice can be found in Asian grocery stores or online. It's different from regular rice, so ensure you're using the correct type for this recipe.
- Adjust the sweetness by adding more or less sugar to the sticky rice according to your preference.
- To toast sesame seeds, heat them in a dry skillet over medium heat, stirring frequently until golden brown and fragrant.

Mango Sticky Rice is a popular Thai dessert known for its creamy texture, fragrant coconut flavor, and sweet mango topping. It's a delightful treat that brings a taste of tropical paradise to your table!

S'mores Dip

Ingredients:

- 1 cup milk chocolate chips
- 1 cup mini marshmallows
- Graham crackers, for serving

Instructions:

1. **Preheat the Oven:**
   - Preheat your oven to 450°F (230°C).
2. **Prepare the Baking Dish:**
   - Spread the chocolate chips evenly in the bottom of a small oven-safe dish or skillet.
3. **Add Marshmallows:**
   - Scatter the mini marshmallows evenly over the chocolate chips, covering them completely.
4. **Bake:**
   - Place the dish or skillet in the preheated oven and bake for 5-7 minutes, or until the marshmallows are golden brown and puffed up.
5. **Serve:**
   - Remove from the oven and let it cool for a few minutes.
   - Serve the S'mores Dip warm with graham crackers for dipping.
6. **Enjoy:**
   - Dip the graham crackers into the gooey chocolate and marshmallow mixture for a delicious S'mores experience!

Tips:

- Keep an eye on the dip while baking to ensure the marshmallows don't burn. They should be golden brown and melted.
- You can also use a broiler for 1-2 minutes to quickly toast the marshmallows, but watch closely to prevent burning.
- Feel free to customize your S'mores Dip by adding toppings like crushed graham crackers, chocolate syrup, or even a drizzle of caramel.

S'mores Dip is a fun and easy dessert that brings the classic flavors of S'mores to any gathering or cozy night in. Enjoy the gooey, chocolatey goodness with friends and family!